That Remarkable
LITTLE LADY OF TENAFLY

Alice Clarke Redfield

Best wishes,
Judy Redfield

Judy Redfield

THE
History
PRESS

Published by The History Press
Charleston, SC
www.historypress.com

First published 2020

Manufactured in the United States

ISBN 9781467145466

Library of Congress Control Number: 2019956035

Notice: The information in this book is true and complete to the best of our knowledge. It is offered without guarantee on the part of the author or The History Press. The author and The History Press disclaim all liability in connection with the use of this book.

Dedicated to the memory of Louise Redfield Levy and John Alden Redfield, without whose enthusiastic support and assistance this book would not have been possible.

CONTENTS

CONTENTS

ACKNOWLEDGEMENTS

It goes without saying that this book could not have been written without the warm encouragement and support of Louise Redfield Levy and John Alden Redfield. Louise contacted the interviewees and scheduled their interviews and granted interviews herself. She also allowed me to copy many documents from her extensive collection of family memorabilia. In addition to hosting me for my interview visit and granting interviews himself, John took me to visit the other interviewees when it was their turn to talk to me. He also helped me take numerous items from Louise's collection to the Tenafly Library for Xeroxing and photographed a number of pictures for me from a family album.

The other interviewees, Dumont Clarke III, Laurence Levy, Katherine Stillman Neandross, Dorothy Redfield, Frances Raymond and Katherine Wadham Swann, were similarly enthusiastic about the project. A detailed list outlining their relationships to Alice Redfield appears at the end of the book. In addition, Dumont Clarke III let me copy his father's diary of his voyage around the world.

Other family members also lent their assistance. Alden Redfield provided the Kirksville album and some other reference materials, in addition to conducting two interviews. Alice Redfield Irizarry gave me her father Chuck's collection of family photographs. Nancy Redfield Carkhuff lent me her collection of photos of the Clarke Redfield family to copy. Her daughter Robin Crawford lent me some more. Dumont Clarke IV, the grandson of Dumont Clarke II, provided me with some useful information regarding his branch of the family.

ACKNOWLEDGEMENTS

The Tenafly Public Library graciously granted permission for me to use some photos given to them from Louise Levy's Collection. The website www.familysearch.org provided access to a wealth of public records: census data, birth, marriage and death records, passport applications, draft registrations and the like, which helped clarify a number of details. The *New York Times* archive also proved to be a valuable resource; Wikipedia articles on various topics added additional data; and eBay dealers in paper, photographic and postcard ephemera produced many useful illustrations. My thanks to them all.

INTRODUCTION

What would it be like to grow up unavoidably very different from virtually everyone else you knew? How should you react? What could you do about it? Such thoughts must have occurred to Alice Clarke (1876–1943) when as a young child she first recognized the fact that she was a dwarf.

People have long been fascinated by dwarves of all types. Such individuals are generally classified into two broad categories. Disproportionate dwarves have bodies that appear misshapen. Sadly, due to their abnormal appearance, many of them have been physically abused and mistreated.

Proportionate dwarves, on the other hand, simply look like much smaller versions of ordinary people. Frequently, they are mistaken for children, or treated more or less as dolls, toys or pets by others. Alice belonged to this second group.

Dwarves have a long history of being put on display for the entertainment of others. Nobles or royalty might choose to act as patrons, keeping a dwarf to entertain their courts. Dwarves have also vied with other human curiosities, on display to the general public either individually or as members of a circus. Such exhibitions, although at times distasteful to those on display, could be an important source of income for such individuals who, due to their size or physical limitations, were not well suited to some other occupations.

Given that their small size was their primary distinguishing feature, proportionate dwarves, to be successful for any length of time in a public career, needed to have strong, outgoing personalities, considerable social skills and usually some talent for performance in activities such as music or dancing. Some became quite famous: Jeffrey Hudson (1619–1681) in the court of Henrietta Maria, the wife of King Charles I of England; the Polish count Joseph Boruwlaski (1739–1837) in both continental Europe and Great Britain; Charles S. Stratton (1838–1883), better known as General Tom Thumb, and his wife, Lavinia Warren (1842–1919), Mrs. Tom Thumb, well known both in the United States and internationally.

Sometimes parents, not knowing quite what to do with their dwarf children, might choose to turn them over to other individuals who then acted as their patrons or promoters. These children frequently began their careers at a young age. Some of the things they were asked to do were "cute" but rather demeaning. As young boys, Jeffrey Hudson,[1] Joseph Boruwlaski[2] and Charles Stratton[3] at one time or another were concealed in an urn or a pie and served up at a banquet table before a number of guests. They then sprang out of the container in military dress and proceeded to march up and down the table, to the surprise and delight of the audience.

Unfortunately, dwarves have also found themselves regarded as something less than human. At one point, Joseph Boruwlaski overheard two scientists seriously discussing breeding him with his similarly short sister as though they were farm animals, and he became understandably very upset.[4] Fortunately, nothing came of this plan.

Unlike those who began their careers as children, Lavinia Warren determined on her own to adopt a public life as a dwarf when she was a young adult. After briefly serving as a schoolteacher, she decided she wanted a lifestyle with more adventure. She spent a couple of years touring on a riverboat on the Mississippi as part of a show with other human oddities. When the Civil War put an end to that project, she then contacted P.T. Barnum in New York and went to work with him.

Histories of the lives of such dwarves often tend to focus on their meetings with famous personages, presidents, kings, queens and various nobles of the countries where they lived or visited and, at times, the rare, costly and ultimately impractical gifts that they frequently received from these personages. Sadly, they often found it necessary to sell these baubles in order to keep roofs over their heads or food on their tables.

While Alice Clarke may not have known anything of the earlier professional proportional dwarves, she certainly would have been aware of the activities of her American contemporaries, Charles Stratton and Lavinia Warren. After Charles Stratton died in 1883, Lavinia Warren

Charles S. Stratton, "General Tom Thumb," as Napoleon, one of his favorite character portrayals. *Author's collection.*

Count Primo Magri and his wife, Lavinia Warren, in front of their store. *Author's collection.*

continued her performing career. She married Count Primo Magri in 1885, another proportionate dwarf she met through Barnum. In the early 1900s, that couple appeared on display during the summers at Coney Island, not very far from where Alice lived, in an attraction called Liliputia. There the public could gawk at some three hundred dwarves hired away from other attractions, living in a village scaled to their size and going about their daily lives.[5] At their home in Middleboro, Massachusetts, the couple operated a small store they called Primo's Pastime, selling snacks, soft drinks and photographs of themselves.[6]

From time to time, on first meeting Alice, people would tell her she ought to join the circus as many other dwarves had done. However, she wanted to live as a person, not as an object on display. She was determined to have a regular lifestyle like her friends and neighbors. Could she do it?

Her story begins with her parents' meeting.

Chapter 1

ALL IN THE FAMILY

T he young man came flying up the stairs of the home at 142 Dean Street, Brooklyn. "Fanny! Fanny! I have something to tell you!" he called. Dumont Clarke had just proposed to Cornelia Ellery, and she had accepted him.[7] At the time, he was living in New York with his older brother, Henry, and his wife, Fanny, while he worked at the American Exchange National Bank. Cornelia was a very attractive young lady, whom he had recently met while she was paying a short visit to friends in the city in the spring of 1869. He promptly decided to court her and persuaded her to stay for an extra month. The evening before her scheduled departure, he finally got up the nerve to propose.[8]

Dumont, born in 1840, was the youngest of three brothers, children of a well-to-do banker in Newport, Rhode Island.[9] The middle brother, William, passed away in 1867. Although Dumont was originally educated for the church, his father's untimely death in 1862[10] led him to forego ordination. Instead, he felt lured by the prospects in California and joined some friends to try his luck in the hardware business there. Unfortunately, that venture did not go well for him, and he soon returned to Newport, entering the bank founded by his grandfather. In 1863, he moved to New York City and took a position as a check clerk at the American Exchange National Bank. By 1868, he had worked his way up to assistant cashier.[11]

Cornelia, born in 1845, also had family ties to Newport, as both her parents were born there. She had come to New York in 1869 on a visit from her family's current home in Castleton, Vermont.[12] Her father, Frank

Ellery, was a navy man and had served many years at sea. He came ashore in 1835 and married a young "Newport Belle," Elizabeth Martin, twenty-one years his junior. Cornelia was their fourth daughter. She, like her siblings, was born in New York, where her father served the U.S. Navy for many years on Naval Courts-Martial, ultimately rising to the rank of commodore. Frank Ellery retired with his family to Castleton in 1855. His family had ties there too, since his maternal uncle Colonel Amos Bird had been the first white man to explore the area and was one of the original settlers in the town. Ellery himself had also spent some time there during his service in the War of 1812.[13]

Dumont and Cornelia were married by a justice of the peace in Castleton, Vermont, on May 20, 1869. The newlyweds' honeymoon trip included some unexpected drama when the train they were riding on stopped at a station in Pennsylvania. There, a mob was chasing a black man. As the man ran toward them, Dumont got off the train. He pulled out a revolver and pointed it at the crowd, holding them at bay.[14]

While one might assume that, given his family background, Dumont would have little to do with others of a lower social station, such was not the case. Even as a young boy, he had enjoyed spending time with people from all walks of life, actually preferring to be with those whose background was different from his own. He had a natural, friendly and outgoing disposition, which never failed to serve him well.[15]

Dumont's business and personal skills soon brought him to the attention of George S. Coe, the president of the American Exchange National Bank, and Coe became his mentor. Meanwhile, the young couple settled in New York City and started their family right away. Their eldest son, Edward Stanley, was born on February 24, 1870. A second son, Lewis Latham, was born in 1871, and a daughter, Mary, in 1872. That same year, with a growing family and a personal preference for country life—and likely with the encouragement of Coe, who had settled in Englewood, New Jersey, earlier—Dumont moved the family to a one-hundred-acre homestead in Schraalenburgh, a small town a short distance to the north of where Coe lived.

It was probably sometime around this move that Dumont and Cornelia noticed that Stanley was not growing like his younger brother and sister. Though perfectly healthy, he was not getting taller at the same rate that they were. Something was clearly amiss, and they did not know what to do about it—not surprising, really, as no one else at that time did either. They resolved to treat him just like their other children as far as possible, assigning him

Clarke family circa 1885. *From left to right are (front row, seated)* Alice, Cornelia, Dumont Jr., Dumont Sr., Corinne and Stanley; *(back row, standing):* Ernest, Lewis and Mary. *Author's collection.*

appropriate chores around the house and sending him off to school when he was old enough.

Awareness of Stanley's condition apparently did not make them wary of continuing to grow their family. A third son, Ernest, was born in 1873.[16] A second daughter, Martha, was born in 1874, but sadly she lived only a few weeks. Two years later, another daughter arrived, and they named her Alice Coe, in honor of her father's mentor. She was followed by Martha, who was born in 1879 but died three years later. Then came Corinne Italia, born in 1881 and finally Dumont Jr. in 1883.[17] The family posed for a group portrait about 1885.

As the children grew older, their parents realized that both Alice and Corinne would be abnormally short as well. At what point the short children realized that they were different from the others is unclear, but it had probably happened by the time they reached school age.

While his family was growing, Dumont's banking career was advancing as well. In 1878, he was appointed cashier. In 1883, he was elected a director

Left: George S. Coe. Unidentified publication. *Author's collection.*

Below: Clarke Greenhouse at "The Chestnuts," Schraalenburgh, New Jersey. *Author's collection.*

of the bank and, in 1887, vice president. After George Coe suffered a paralytic stroke,[18] Dumont became president of the American Exchange National Bank in 1894. Never one to play politics, his advancement occurred simply on a basis of merit.[19]

Coe had played a key role in the American banking industry throughout his career. During the Civil War, he developed a plan to deal with the North's financial difficulties that he persuaded Secretary of the Treasury Salmon P. Chase and major New York, Boston and Philadelphia bankers to successfully adopt. In the 1880s, he was able to avert a major banking crisis in New York by developing a similar plan.[20]

Dumont Clarke followed in his mentor's footsteps at the bank. But when the directors wanted to reward him with an increase in salary, he turned them down, claiming that he was not worth what they were paying him already, and he had no wish for the bank to own him.[21]

In 1883, he had purchased the William C. Browning estate, "The Chestnuts," the property adjacent to his original Schraalenburgh home on the east. Besides a substantial residence, the property boasted a large greenhouse, a strong attraction for one with horticultural interests. Dumont Clarke sold his former home and five acres surrounding it to Charles R. Osborn, a wine merchant.[22]

The greenhouse provided fresh fruits and vegetables for the family as well as flowers out of season. Strawberries and grapes were plentiful.[23] The grapes in particular were prized by family and friends alike.[24] Dumont indulged his passion for growing roses there,[25] along with lilies and violets.[26] As they grew older, the girls would go and sit in the greenhouse with their beaus when they came calling of a Sunday afternoon.[27]

Dumont seemed intent on keeping his business and home lives separate. He made no real attempt to take part in New York society, though the banking business put him in constant contact with its members. For years, he refused to have a telephone installed at home. While he seemed to see his home as a refuge for himself, at the same time, the family was encouraged to entertain friends and relatives.[28]

Family life was generally warm and caring. But family members were not above playing pranks on one another from time to time. Young Stanley enjoyed hunting. So when Dumont decided to smear currant jelly on Stanley's face and add buckshot to the mixture, the result was quite horrifying for the ladies of the family. His wife and daughters and the housekeeper refused to speak with him for a week. However, during that week, the ladies were not idle. Dumont was scheduled to attend a board meeting at the bank, an occasion

Cornelia Clarke and her parrots. *John Redfield.*

requiring formal dress. They cut grotesque figures out of newspapers and surreptitiously attached them to his coattails. During the meeting, he saw the other board members regarding him strangely. Finally, an office boy could control himself no longer and burst into helpless laughter, pointing to the additions to his wardrobe. When he discovered the prank, Dumont had to pause the meeting until he could contain his own mirth.[29]

Cornelia spent much of her time at home with her large family, although she did go on trips to visit friends and relatives on occasion. Fortunately, her husband was able to provide her with the services of a cook and a maid to assist her. She herself was a good cook[30] and likely passed her skills on to her daughters as well. Her taste in furnishings was quite elaborate and fussy in the then current Victorian style.[31] She also had a liking for exotic pets. At one point, she adopted a monkey, and there were a couple of parrots as well.[32]

Unfortunately, Cornelia frequently felt unwell. Whether she was truly ill or feeling put upon by her family responsibilities is unclear.[33] Perhaps she suffered from migraines. Whatever the cause, she took to dosing herself with a variety of patent medicines and saved them all, partially used or not.[34] She had a strong interest in all things medical.

The abnormal shortness of Stanley, Alice and Corinne was not the only serious medical issue among the children. Ernest suffered from epilepsy,[35] and the family sent him away periodically to various medical institutions and spas, even once as far away as Germany[36] in search of a successful form of treatment. Sadly, none of these efforts proved effective.

Although Henry Clarke and his family lived in New York while Dumont's family lived in New Jersey, the two families remained close. The two brothers shared ownership of some family property in Jamestown, Rhode Island, and both visited there with their children in the summer. Stanley and Alice particularly enjoyed being in Rhode Island and sometimes stayed there with their cousins on their own.[37] Henry's younger children and Dumont's older children were similar in age. Alice and Henry's daughter Jessie became lifelong friends and wrote each other frequently when they were apart.

By the early 1890s, Dumont's older children were entering adulthood. Stanley, though basically friendly and good-natured, was also considered a bit wild. His short stature likely made him subject to teasing and bullying from other boys, which did not help the situation. His parents sent him to a military school, St. Paul's in Garden City, Long Island, hoping that would help him develop more self-discipline.[38]

Lewis began his education at a private school in Englewood, New Jersey. For a time, he attended the public school in Schraalenburgh and then went on to take a business course at Packard Institute in New York. In 1889, he followed his father into the American Exchange National Bank, starting as an office boy and working his way up through the ranks.[39]

Believing that more than a basic education was important for women as well as men, the Clarkes sent Mary to a finishing school, the Bordentown Female College in Bordentown, New Jersey. She did well there but left before her senior year. The principal reportedly told her she would have been at the head of her class if she had stayed.[40]

Meanwhile, the younger children were still in school at home. Corinne, a somewhat introverted personality, tended to be more sensitive and easily offended than the others and regarded her short stature as a significant burden. Dumont Jr. was a good natured individual, laid back, friendly and outgoing, who gradually developed into the family peacemaker.

And then there was Alice.

Chapter 2

GROWING UP ALICE

Not a great deal is known about the details of Alice's early life, though a number of photographs from that period survive. Even as an infant, she radiated an intensity and determination that characterized her life. At the same time, she embodied a warm outgoing personality like her father. From the time she was a young child, she realized that she would have to face the fact that she would always be small, and there was nothing she could do about it.[41]

During her early years, like other young children, Alice enjoyed simple childhood pleasures. When visiting her Uncle Henry's home in New York, she spent a lot of time looking out the window watching all the traffic, enjoying the vastly different scene from that around her country home. When visiting the family property in Jamestown, she particularly liked opening and closing the gates along the road for people to pass through the fields on the way to the nearby lighthouse.[42]

One task she had at home was to go around every evening after all the lights were out and check all the downstairs fireplaces, to be sure that there were no stray sparks that might catch the house on fire. Since the house had been broken into on various occasions, she was quite anxious while she did this, and she walked backward up the stairs when she had finished, concerned about avoiding a potential surprise attack. In later years, she viewed this task as an effort by her father to help her learn to overcome fear.[43]

As she grew older, Alice became the go-to person in the family when someone was ill or needed assistance. She was the one who helped her mother through her many illnesses[44] and helped with Ernest—both assisting

Left: Alice as an infant. *Author's collection*; *Right*: Alice as a young teen. *Alice Irizarry.*

with his needs while he was at home and keeping in touch with him while he was away.[45] "Let Alice do it!" became a common family theme.[46]

Having completed her basic education at home, at age sixteen she followed in her sister Mary's footsteps, enrolling in Bordentown Female College, in Bordentown, New Jersey. The school was located on a scenic bluff overlooking the Delaware River, in a building dating back to the Revolutionary War that had reportedly once served as the residence of the activist Thomas Payne.[47]

Although termed a "college," in reality it appears to have functioned essentially as a finishing school. It was founded during the Civil War by the Reverend John H. Brakeley and, at that time, clearly offered only a finishing school curriculum: English, French, Latin, drawing, painting, vocal music and piano.[48]

By 1880, the school had been taken over by the Reverend William C. Bowen and developed a good reputation under his leadership, apparently continuing in the finishing school mode, offering classes in such subjects as music, French and elocution.[49] Alice's parents were pleased with Mary's experiences there and happy to have Alice attend as well. She and her cousin Jessie Clarke enrolled in the school in the fall of 1892 and stayed through the spring of 1893.

Unfortunately, by that time, conditions at the school had significantly changed. Reverend Bowen passed away in 1890. His wife, Gertrude, attempted to keep the school going, but apparently, she was neither a good administrator nor a good disciplinarian, and the girls quickly learned that they could do pretty much as they pleased. At one point, she threatened to send all of them home in disgrace as the result of some infraction, then failed to carry out her threat. One of the girls decided not to show up for class one day, and when sent for, she simply sent back word that she couldn't come because she was "dressing." When Mrs. Bowen received an unpleasant anonymous letter and Jessie told her that the principal of her former school simply threw such things in the trash, she put her head down on her desk and cried.[50]

Whenever the students went for their daily walks around town, Jessie and Alice preferred to be at the end of the line, so that they might flirt with any of the boys from the neighboring Bordentown Military Academy who happened to come by. Sometimes in the evenings they might let down notes on strings from their bedroom window, much to the annoyance of the French teacher whose room was directly below theirs.[51] At one point, they even threw a midnight party in their room, complete with an invitation written on a piece of wallpaper listing the various goodies available. The school could not long continue to function in such an uncontrolled manner, and it closed later in the year.

Alice's parents decided to continue her education closer to home, at the Dwight School for Girls in Englewood, New Jersey. Named for the then president of Yale University, the Reverend Timothy Dwight V, it was founded in 1889 by two women, Euphemia S. Creighton and Ellen W. Farrar,[52] and unlike Bordentown, served as both a college preparatory and a finishing school. It offered a much broader spectrum of subjects than Bordentown had, including such topics as algebra, geometry, chemistry, physiology, botany, geology, geography, astronomy, history, natural history, natural philosophy, moral science and mental science, in addition to the more basic finishing school subjects: English, drawing, art history, French, German and Latin.[53] Intended primarily for day students, it accepted some boarders as well.[54] Alice attended as a day student in 1894 and 1895 and followed an essentially finishing school–type curriculum, although in her final quarter she did study algebra and geography.[55]

In order to get to school each day, Alice had to take the train from the nearby town of Cresskill. Why Cresskill when she lived in Schraalenburgh? The Clarke home was situated near the midpoint of a plateau approximately

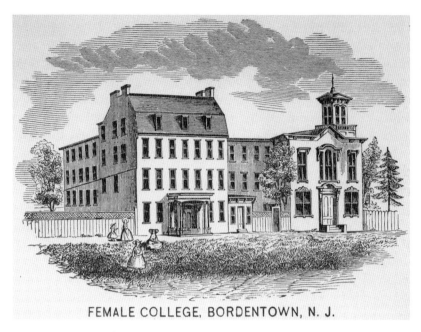

FEMALE COLLEGE, BORDENTOWN, N. J.

Bordentown Female College, Bordentown, New Jersey. Vignette from a receipt. *Author's collection.*

A portion of the Midnight Party Menu. *Louise Redfield Levy.*

equidistant from the centers of both Schraalenburgh and Cresskill, each of which was served by a different railroad. The one passing through Cresskill was the one that would take her closest to the school.

Alice was not the only person trying to catch that train in the morning. One of the Clarkes' neighbors who lived just across the street was punctilious and a stickler about schedules. Everything he did had to be timed just so. His coachman would stand at the foot of the stairs, and he would stand on his front porch with his watch in his hand, and at exactly such and such a time, whatever it was, he'd rush down the steps, jump into the wagon and they would tear down the hill to the Cresskill station to catch the train. And the conductor at the bottom, and the engineer, and everybody in the train of course would stand there and time it, and when the scheduled departure time was reached the conductor would signal, and away they'd go—there was much cheering if he didn't make it.

Alice would usually start early and be there. But one day, she wasn't down the hill yet, and she was coming. And they could see her coming, and they could see the wagon coming down the hill, and they held the train until she reached it and practically threw her on, but they still got away before he arrived. Alice was always careful after that to start early so that she wouldn't be the one who had caused him to catch the train because they waited for her.[56]

A family friend and fellow student, Frances Leggett, came down from her home in Nyack on the same commuter train. Alice would ride down the three stops to Englewood with her, and the two would then walk up the hill to the school together.[57] Much later, Frances Leggett became principal of the school and ran it for many years.[58]

Alice was also a close friend of her next-door neighbors, the Worth family. Like the Clarkes, they had a large number of children. The Worths hailed originally from Wilmington, North Carolina, but had moved to the New York area, where the father, Archibald Worth, worked as a corn merchant. Two of the girls, Elizabeth "Lizzie" Worth and Jessie Worth, were similar in age to Alice and became close friends of hers. Members of the two families constantly visited back and forth.

The Worths' southern relatives periodically came north for a visit, and Alice got to know them as well. William Worth, the oldest son, had trained as a lawyer. When he married, he moved back south to Petersburg, Virginia, just outside of Richmond—close to where his wife's family lived. Over the years, Alice made a number of trips to visit with his family in Petersburg and the others in Wilmington, North Carolina, as well.

Dwight School for Girls, Englewood, New Jersey. *Author's collection.*

Cresskill Railroad Station, Cresskill, New Jersey. *Author's collection.*

Because she knew her size would inevitably attract people's attention Alice always wanted to be well dressed, though not conspicuously. All her clothes had to be specially made. For everyday wear, she did much of the basic sewing herself but had a local dressmaker add the finishing touches. For elegant, more formal clothes, she went to a dressmaker in New York. In addition to garments, handkerchiefs, gloves and even jewelry had to be specially made appropriate to her size.

Shoes were another problem. As a young adult, she had to wear children's shoes in children's styles. She finally discovered the Footsaver Company, which was willing to make her adult-style shoes to fit her child size 13 feet. They made a special last for her. One time, the person taking her order at the company mistakenly had her shoes made up in an adult size 13 instead. Undismayed, the firm displayed matching pairs of the shoes in both sizes in its show window, to demonstrate the shoemakers' versatility.[59]

Alice made friends easily and maintained many friendships throughout her life. How did she do it? Knowing people would be surprised and even shocked by her size when they first met her, and wouldn't know what to say, or what to do, she always made a point of putting them at ease. She would say something like, "What a lovely dress you have on," or "How well you look today." She firmly believed one should never be self-conscious. "If you're self-conscious, it's because you're thinking too much about yourself. You're being too self-centered. Think about the other person and try to put them at ease."[60]

Nevertheless, there were some uncomfortable moments. When a new beau came to visit her sister Mary, even when Alice was in her late teens, she sometimes found herself being picked up and placed on his lap, as though she were a young child.[61]

Alice was an attractive young lady, and young men were not averse to courting her as well. One young man, Eugene Woodward, a Worth relative from Wilmington, North Carolina, who had met Alice on one of his family's visits north, could not forget her. In the manner of the time, he wrote first to her mother to obtain permission to write to her, and then sent her a letter expressing his attraction. She wrote him back a friendly letter but told him to stop flirting.[62] Nevertheless they remained on good terms.

Like her mother, Alice was fond of animals. A friend gave her a pet canary in 1890, and she enjoyed its singing for many years.[63] Somewhat surprisingly, despite her size, she got along well with the family's large dogs, which were kept in part as deterrents for potential burglars.

Alice at age nineteen. Kirksville Album. *Author's collection.*

Just as Cornelia kept searching for a successful treatment for her son Ernest's epilepsy, she also looked for a possible way to help her short children grow to a more normal height. She learned of a doctor in Kirksville, Missouri, who might have a solution and decided to send Alice and Corinne there to see what he could do.

Chapter 3

THE KIRKSVILLE ADVENTURE

The innovative doctor Cornelia had heard about was Andrew Taylor Still. Although born in Tennessee, he had spent the early part of his life in the state of Kansas. During the Civil War, he served as a medical steward and often as a de facto surgeon. After his first wife died in 1860, and three of his children died of spinal meningitis in 1864, he decided that medicine as it was then currently practiced had many shortcomings. Nevertheless, he took a short course in medicine at the College of Physicians and Surgeons in Kansas City, Missouri, which he completed in 1870.

He soon rejected the traditional medical practices of the early nineteenth century, such as bleeding, purging and dosing individuals with either poisonous compounds, such as mercurous chloride, or addictive ones like opium and alcohol. He regarded the human body as being perfect, functioning as a total biological unit, including self-healing and self-regulatory mechanisms and interrelated structures and functions. If abnormal pressures and strains occurred on one part of the body, the result would be abnormal pressures and strains on other parts. He believed that the use of manipulative therapy, rather than medications, would work to release the body's healing powers.[64] He called his method osteopathy, derived from the Greek words *osteon* for "bone" and *pathos* for "suffering."

Between 1874 and 1892. he spent much of his time traveling from town to town in Missouri explaining his views to anyone who would listen, carrying a bag of bones to illustrate his points and gradually developing a following. He obtained a charter for his American School of Osteopathy in Kirksville on May 10, 1892. His first class included five of his children, his daughter Blanche being one. Still saw no reason why women should not learn what he had to teach, and that first class included five women. The class lasted for a period of four months, and Still was unhappy with the results. Four months proved to be insufficient time to do the necessary training, and there was a shortage of materials to provide adequate anatomy lessons.[65]

Some local doctors called Still a quack and feared that their practices would be ruined by his activities, but his patients enthusiastically praised his treatments, which produced many positive results.[66] Soon, people from all over the country and from all walks of life were flocking to Kirksville in hopes that Still might be able to help them.

In the fall of 1894, Still began his second class, which consisted of thirty students. This time, students were enrolled for a period of eighteen months, and they were required to earn a grade of at least 90 percent in their course in anatomy.[67]

At the same time, he had been working to develop a quality permanent home for his school. With the help of his brother Thomas, who designed the building, and other investors, the A.T. Still Infirmary was constructed and officially dedicated on January 10, 1895. The three-story building was lit with electric light and had an electric bell system in every room. Seven operating rooms were located on the ground floor. The secretary's office and a ladies' waiting room were situated on the second floor. The lecture room, called Memorial Hall, provided seating for up to two hundred people.[68]

Alice and Corinne arrived in Kirksville in January 1896. But where was Stanley? Tired of his eldest son's tendency to fool around and get into mischief, Dumont Clarke had decided to place him in a position where he would be under supervision and have to act more responsibly. On November 15, 1894, Stanley embarked on a voyage around the world on a merchant sailing ship, the *S.P. Hitchcock*, which was still in progress.

The Clarke sisters stayed in Kirksville from January to May 1896. While no written record is available for their visit, a detailed photographic record exists, thanks to the efforts of William Watson Meade from Grand Rapids, Michigan, who produced a special album for Alice containing 109 pictures about her time there. Meade appears to have been one of the members in the ongoing osteopathy class, presumably the third class of students. What makes this album particularly valuable are the written notes accompanying each picture, listing the people shown and the events that took place.

The treatment Dr. Still prescribed for the two girls included giving them what was described as a thyroid medication. It reportedly helped them

A.T. Still Infirmary, Kirksville, Missouri, 1896. Kirksville Album. *Author's collection.*

A manipulative therapy treatment room in the infirmary. Kirksville Album. *Author's collection.*

grow a little but caused such severe headaches that Alice ceased taking it, although she continued with the adjustment treatments, finding they enhanced her feeling of well-being. She spent the rest of her time in Kirksville enjoying the visit.[69]

Unlike what happens in modern medical facilities, patients, students, teachers and members of the Still family interacted socially with one another on a regular basis, no doubt as a result of the extended time they all spent together. The patients present at that time ranged from a young boy on crutches to some elderly ladies in wheelchairs. Such patients were often accompanied by family members or servants who assisted them in getting around.

One of Alice's particular friends was Albert Hansen, a young man confined to a wheelchair who lived with his mother in a home near the infirmary. Alice also became close friends with the Charles Still family. She specially enjoyed their young daughter Gladys, who was a toddler at the time. Alice loved children and was particularly able to relate to them, no doubt aided by her small size.

Parties and picnics were frequently arranged in which everyone who chose to would take part. Alice helped organize and prepare for some of these events. When she was light-heartedly given a "Tin Cup and Plate Award" for her efforts, in the same spirit she regally displayed her trophy.

And then there were occasions when people simply enjoyed fooling around. Dr. Still's demonstrator skeleton, which he had named "Columbus," was termed "Our Mutual Friend" by students and patients and at times figured in such events. Even members of the Still family sometimes joined in.

The only time that Alice appears to have felt a bit ill at ease is in a portrait with Dr. Still himself.

Corrine, on the other hand, appears in the pictures as much more retiring. She is usually near the back of a group in a photo, like in the picture with Albert Hansen, and she never seems to smile, even in a close-up portrait by herself.

Cornelia came to Kirksville in May to pick up the girls, and while she was there, the three of them posed for a formal portrait together taken by a local professional photographer named Parcell. In it, he minimized their differences in size by having Corinne and Cornelia sit at different heights while Alice stood beside them. While photographs of professional dwarves typically emphasized their size difference from other people, Clarke family photos, like this one, generally were arranged so that the size difference was less obvious.

Alice (*far right*) with Albert Hansen and a group of friends. Corinne sits in the background. Kirksville Album. *Author's collection.*

Alice comforting Gladys Still after she was startled by her family's dog Duke. Kirksville Album. *Author's collection.*

Alice with a wheelbarrow load prepared for the "Tin Cup" Picnic. Kirksville Album. *Author's collection.*

Alice with the "Tin Cup and Plate" Award. Kirksville Album. *Author's collection.*

"Our Mutual Friend" with his pipe relaxing on a bench. Kirksville Album. *Author's collection.*

Alice and Blanche Still fooling around on the infirmary porch. Kirksville Album. *Author's collection.*

Dr. A.T. Still and Alice Clarke. Kirksville Album. *Author's collection.*

Corinne sitting on porch steps. Kirksville Album. *Author's collection.*

Corinne, Cornelia and Alice Clarke in Kirksville. *Tenafly Public Library.*

Alice stayed in contact with the friends she made in Kirksville for a number of years. William Meade sent her the Kirksville album in 1901. In 1902, Dr. Charles Still and his wife, Anna, stopped by Alice's home in New Jersey,[70] and she wrote to Albert Hansen, among others, during her trip to Europe in 1903.[71]

Chapter 4

BACK HOME

M eanwhile, back in Schraalenburgh changes had been taking place. In 1894, the New Jersey legislature had passed a law combining all the formerly independent school districts in the state into single districts for each township and requiring all residents of the township to be responsible not only for the combined debts of all the former districts—not just their own—but also for all debts incurred in the future by the new township district. However, a law passed in 1878 exempted incorporated boroughs, towns, villages and cities from this rule. Having no desire to be saddled with other peoples' debts, the leaders of the borough of Schraalenburgh decided to incorporate, as did the neighboring boroughs in Palisade County, Bergenfield, Tenafly and Cresskill. There was no unincorporated space left between their borders.

Schraalenburgh's petition for incorporation was approved by the courts, and a vote was held on the issue on July 19, 1894. The vote passed, and Schraalenburgh became an incorporated borough on July 20. On August 28, 1894, Dumont Clarke was elected the first mayor of the town, for a one-year term. He was reelected twice more. The first annual appropriation for the borough was $200, which Clarke personally loaned to it until taxes could be collected. All meetings of the first mayor and council were held at the Clarke home.[72]

At about the same time, developers from the New York area "discovered" northern New Jersey as an ideal location for residential development away from the disadvantages of city living. One such company thought it would

Dumont Clarke Sr. *Robin Crawford.*

be a good idea to get rid of the old odd Dutch name for the town and change it to "Kensington" instead, as that sounded more distinguished. Dumont Clarke and other prominent citizens opposed the move. On June 13, 1898, while he and his wife were away on a world tour, the mayor and council voted instead to change the name of the borough to Dumont. When he learned of the change, he accepted the honor graciously but noted that he still preferred the old name.[73]

Meanwhile, on November 15, 1894, Stanley had embarked on his trip around the world on the sailing vessel *S.P. Hitchcock.* He was booked as a passenger on the ship, which left New York Harbor that day bound for Yokohama, Japan. He took along a variety of items for the trip, among them books to read, nautical charts, a notebook to use as a diary, a telescope to help see the sights, a banjo for entertainment and a small personal supply of whiskey, which he ended up sharing with the captain and some other crew members on occasion.

Life onboard ship was somewhat Spartan. After the first few days, only preserved foods were available to eat, unless someone succeeded in catching some fish. Because the fresh water supply was limited, bathing was virtually impossible, and doing laundry was only a possibility when those on board were able to capture enough rainwater during a storm. Supplies needed for any routine maintenance activities had to be already on board. Depending on wind and weather conditions, sailors' work might be intense at some times and rather slack at others. Any injuries or illnesses that occurred received limited treatment based on what was available in the ship's medicine chest. Spending long periods of time in the inevitable close quarters aboard ship led at times to the breakout of sharp disagreements and periodic fights among members of the crew.

The voyage to Yokohama took 134 days, reaching that port on March 29, 1895. During the trip, Stanley learned how to "shoot the sun" with a sextant and plot the ship's course on a chart. He also spent a fair amount of time up in the rigging with his telescope, checking out other ships and landmarks they passed. While rounding the Cape of Good Hope, he accidentally dropped the telescope from on high to the deck below, damaging it severely.

In Yokohama, he was happy to go ashore to do some sightseeing and buy souvenirs, as well as to have a chance to eat some fresh fruits and vegetables and drink some fresh milk for a change. He visited a Buddhist temple and attended the Union Church where Europeans worshiped, noting it was the size of the Presbyterian Church back home in Tenafly. In Nagasato, he enjoyed the hot sulfur baths and admired the scenery. On a visit to Tokyo, he noticed apple trees espaliered the same way he had seen grape vines treated at home.

Back in Yokohama, he got to tally the loading of ballast into the ship. He went with the captain to visit other captains in port and listen to their sailing yarns. He even took part in a yacht race in which his crew was the winner.

The ship finally began loading cargo for the next leg of the voyage on June 4, 1895, about two months after its arrival. Various sized lots of tea and curios arrived from time to time over the next month. On July 10, 1895, they set sail for San Francisco, arriving there on August 8.

The *S.P. Hitchcock*'s stay in San Francisco was much shorter. All the cargo for that port was unloaded in a week. During the next two weeks while he was there, Stanley attended a number of plays and enjoyed visits to a Turkish bath. He walked in Golden Gate Park and hired a buggy to take him out to see Cliff House. He even managed a brief visit to a mechanics fair that was going on at the time. On August 28, the ship set sail for Honolulu.

When the crew arrived in Honolulu on September 14, 1895, they found the city was in the midst of a cholera outbreak, and the ship was placed in quarantine for a few days. Over the next few weeks, they were in and out of quarantine in response to new cholera outbreaks but managed to go ashore and see the sights on occasion, including Mauna Loa and Waikiki Beach. The crew spent time unloading ballast at first. Later, between quarantine periods, dockworkers began loading sugar into the hold. Stanley found the native people friendly. Groups frequently came out to visit the boat, and when they could go ashore, he and the captain were entertained at many luaus and hulas. The native women were most hospitable.

In early November, when quarantine was finally lifted, Stanley and some friends left on a three-day tour on an island steamer to visit a couple of sugar plantations and a rice plantation. They saw a sugar mill at one location, but the highlight of the trip for him was the opportunity to go hunting in the fields. He managed to bag two dozen plovers and a duck. When the group got back to the *Hitchcock*, it was getting ready to leave, but not before a couple of big farewell luau parties were held. The voyage back to New York began on November 7, 1895.

Their course took them through the south Pacific and around Cape Horn. Being so far south during the southern summer meant they had only about one hour of darkness at night. They had to pass through fields of icebergs, which made the captain nervous. During this portion of the trip, they encountered a couple of severe storms that flooded the decks and cabins and threw their contents all around. During one storm, half the sails were ripped to shreds.

Stanley found himself serving as the medical officer of the ship, doing what he could with the contents of the medicine chest, but not really knowing what needed doing. He tried putting iodine on the cheek of a man who was suffering a toothache, which obviously didn't help. Another sailor complained of an ache in his side. After trying three different remedies on him without success, he determined the fellow was actually malingering, trying to get out of the maintenance job of "tarring down" because he didn't like the smell of the hot tar. The ship finally reached New York on March 13, 1896, 127 days after leaving Honolulu. While Stanley had enjoyed much of the trip, he was happy to be back home. He subsequently went to work as a clerk in a brokerage office.[74]

Meanwhile, those who had remained home continued much as before. Lewis continued working at the bank. From his original position as office boy, he was soon promoted to messenger and subsequently served for five years as secretary to the president, his father. About 1900, he was promoted to assistant cashier. He had also entered the New York National Guard and spent ten years there, rising to the position of captain of his troop while continuing his banking career.[75] As a member of the National Guard, he went to Washington in 1893 to take part in Grover Cleveland's second inauguration.[76]

Ernest's epilepsy found him spending more and more time away from home in search of treatment and a cure. In the fall of 1896, he spent a while at an institution in Bielefeld, Germany, and his family wrote to him there. Alice sent him copies of the *New York World* newspaper so he could follow the details of the presidential election that year.[77]

Mary and Alice, having completed their formal education, were living at home, as was Corinne. Unlike her older sisters, there appears to be no evidence of Corinne ever attending a finishing school. Young Dumont was still in school and beginning to think seriously about going into the ministry.

What was the life of a young well-to-do single lady like at the turn of the twentieth century? Since there was no need for her to go to work outside the home, Alice spent part of her time helping out with household chores. For her, these involved a good deal of sewing and mending. She also did food preparation on occasion, ranging from everyday tasks like churning butter to special ones like making sandwiches, candy or ice cream for particular events. If the regular help was away, she might even prepare a full meal or do some housecleaning.

When her mother was ill, she took care of her, and when Ernest had problems, she dealt with some of those situations as well. When not busy with other chores, Alice enjoyed reading good current popular novels, many of which are considered classics to this day. Photography was a particular interest of hers—not just taking pictures but developing and printing them as well. With Corinne, she would often play various board games, including Halma, from which Chinese Checkers evolved.[78]

In the early 1900s, only Alice and Dumont Jr. attended church regularly. Although her diaries never say which church, it most likely was the Presbyterian Church in Tenafly. When looking for a comparison for the Yokohama church he visited, Stanley used that church as an example. While Alice was visiting in the South in 1902, she joined the Presbyterian Church, and Dumont Jr. decided to go to college to train to be a Presbyterian minister.

Alice also enjoyed an active social life. Young people from the neighboring boroughs, boys and girls, frequently got together. Clarkes from Dumont,

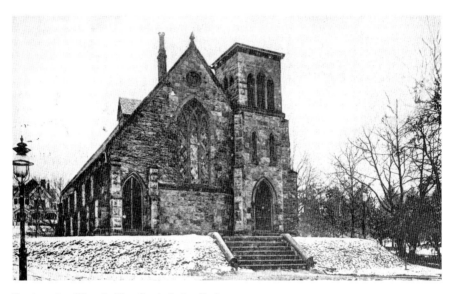

Presbyterian Church, Tenafly. *Author's collection.*

Alice with a group of friends at the dunes on the Jersey Shore. *John Redfield.*

Worths from Cresskill, Dakins from Tenafly and Redfields from Closter often made up part of the group.

Dancing was one of Alice's favorite activities. Playing lawn tennis or table tennis were others. Occasionally, she even played tetherball or pool. Rowing a boat was something else she liked to do. Although she did not ride a horse, she traveled around the area in her pony cart. While the family groom normally took care of that for her, if need be, she knew how to harness or unharness the pony herself.[79]

The pony was a bit temperamental and not always easy to manage. On at least one occasion, he overturned the cart, and on another, he managed to throw Alice right out of it in the middle of Jay Street in Tenafly. One of the residents nearby picked her up and drove her to the home of another, where the gardener had caught the runaway. Fortunately, Alice was uninjured. She was more concerned that her family at home not find out about the mishap and not at all deterred from taking out the pony cart the next day.[80]

Almost every day, Alice went to visit friends, or they came to visit her. At times, she might host a luncheon for a few of them or attend one at another friend's house. Card parties also were a popular form of local entertainment. She belonged to a choral group that met weekly in Tenafly and presented a concert in the spring. She also enjoyed attending plays and operas in New York with family and friends.[81] All in all, her lifestyle differed little from that of her friends of normal size.

Chapter 5

ROMANCE BEGINS TO BLOOM

Before long, members of Alice's group of friends began to pair off. Among the first to do so were Belle Dakin from Tenafly and Edwin Redfield from Closter. When they married in 1897, Alice served as one of Belle's bridesmaids.[82]

Then Alice's sister Mary became engaged to George B. Case, a young up-and-coming lawyer in New York City who lived in Schraalenburgh like the Clarkes.[83] Mary was the apple of her father's eye, and he had big plans for her wedding. But Mary and her husband-to-be had a different idea. Instead of a fancy wedding with a lot of fuss, they decided to marry quietly on their own.[84] The ceremony, held in the Church of the Incarnation in New York on March 11, 1898, was very informal, with only a few relatives and friends attending, officially reported as due to concerns regarding the bride's health.[85] The couple left immediately on an extended trip to Europe. For the next few days, the clerks in the bank were busy addressing the announcements.[86] The Cases' first child, Mary Ermine, named for her mother and her paternal grandfather, was born on July 5, 1899.[87]

George got to know Alice along with the rest of the Clarke family when he began courting Mary early in 1897. Before long, the two of them had become close friends. In November of that year, he wrote in a letter to her,

You are a dear good girl and I tell you your friendship has meant a great big heap to me these past eight months, and I do want it to go on increasing. So let me try to make it so, won't you? And if I do things you don't like, tell me of it.

Later on in the same missive, he gives a tongue-in-cheek self-evaluation:

I probably am one of the greatest lawyers in New York City. It will not take long for New York to find this important fact out. My clients will number legions and my fees in the tens of thousands. Then we will all take a Mediterranean trip on our steam yacht, surrounded by all our liveried servants and the luxury of unlimited wealth. Will you go? Thank you, you do me great honor.[88]

He did, in fact, become a highly successful lawyer and took care of the Clarke family's legal interests for a number of years. In another letter, George describes his efforts at political campaigning in the late nineteenth century:

We've been having a good deal of fun and excitement in our campaigning. We have a big two horse dray decorated with bunting and appropriate emblems, and a brass band of six red-coated torries [sic] whose music is excruciating. We go over on to 8th Ave. Stop at a corner—play a few tunes, burn a red light—so, and after gathering a crowd get upon the wagon and spout all sorts of stuff. Call [the opposition candidates] all the bad names we can think of, praise Law and Liberty—then move on to the next corner. Tiresome, but good practice.[89]

About this same time, Alice too developed a strong romantic attachment. Her beau was Ed Dakin, one of Belle Dakin's brothers. They attended a number of social events together and seemed to get along well. Certainly, Alice was quite convinced that she had found someone who might be a life partner. Ed Dakin appears to have had other ideas. However the situation came about, in late 1899, they broke up. No record of the reason for the breakup is available, but Alice felt bitterly betrayed. Her 1900 diary has two quotes written on the back flyleaf: "The sin that neither God nor man can forgive, Hypocrisy—Tennyson," and "Oh! What a tangled web we weave when first we practice to deceive."[90] Multiple entries in that diary also mention destroying letters, perhaps ones from him.

Since the Clarke family had no telephone, a lot of communication with neighbors and friends was done through the mail, a fairly efficient method in actuality. At that time, a letter mailed in New York City in the morning would reach the recipient in northern New Jersey in the afternoon and vice versa.

After the breakup, Alice basically did her best to carry on with her everyday life as before, although she was desperately unhappy. Ed still came by to visit occasionally, and she paid occasional visits to the Dakin family, often when he was not around. But in spite of putting a good face on things, at times she was clearly depressed. A portion of her February 17, 1900 diary entry reads, "No one seems to care about me. This certainly is a hard life. Wish it was soon to end." Fortunately, this mood did not last too long.

It may have been at about this time that Alice decided to start planning what she might do if she never did marry. Having children and working with children were important to her, so she determined that in that case she would start an orphanage and perhaps get Corinne to take part in the project with her. She talked over her plans in some detail with her father. "She knew little children liked her and she knew she had some money. She wanted children and she wanted to make people happy and she wanted to be useful."[91]

By that time, she was actively working with children. In 1892, J. Hull Browning had purchased the Westervelt home on Tenafly Road in Tenafly to use as a facility for the underprivileged. He called it the Rethmore Home. Initially, it served as a place to teach practical courses to young women, but it soon became more focused on providing a fresh-air experience for underprivileged children from the city.[92] By the late 1890s Alice was doing volunteer work there. Her efforts were greatly appreciated. Browning presented her with a small diamond-studded pin in the shape of a deer because she was "a little dear."[93]

Rethmore Home. *Author's collection.*

Alice greatly enjoyed singing, and she joined a choral group that met in Tenafly weekly from fall through spring. The exact location of the meetings is unclear, but quite possibly it was at the Rethmore Home as well. Other local young people, including Jessie Worth and Henry Redfield, belonged to the group.

Perhaps as much for a temporary escape from unhappy memories as well as a chance to visit old friends, on April 20, 1900, Alice traveled south to visit the Worth relatives. She spent part of her time in Petersburg, Virginia, where Jessie's brother William Worth and his wife, Lutie, lived, attending parties, a concert and a baseball game while she was there, as well as helping out around the house. Then it was on to Wilmington, North Carolina, to visit with the Worth cousins and their friends, where in addition to the usual social activities, she toured a cotton press and an ice factory. On returning to Petersburg, she went to see what remained of Fort's Hell (the North's) and Damnation (the South's) from the Civil War siege of Richmond in 1864. She returned home on June 14, 1900, just a week before her friend Lizzie Worth's wedding.

Lizzie Worth was marrying Walter Stillman, one of Henry Redfield's closest friends, and Alice helped the Worth family out with the preparations. Everyone had a good time at the wedding rehearsal and the party afterward, and the wedding itself on June 21 went off without a hitch.[94] The newlywed Stillmans established their home in Tenafly, and Alice or Henry Redfield or both would frequently visit them on their way to or from choral practice, sometimes staying for dinner or even spending the night.[95]

On August 11, 1900, Alice traveled to Far Rockaway on Long Island, a summer beachfront vacation spot, where she joined George and Mary and the baby in a cottage that the family was renting. There she spent her time ocean bathing, reading and minding Mary Ermine while the child's parents went house hunting in New York.

The Cases found a house that they liked on West Seventy-Fourth Street, so they all spent three days in September packing things up in Far Rockaway and then three more unloading it all at the new home. Alice stayed on with them, helping them get further settled in until November 1, 1900.[96]

Lewis was the next member of the Clarke family to marry. He chose Florence Kenzel, the daughter of a sea captain, for his bride. Both of them were very much involved in New York high society. She had been in rather poor health while they were courting and went out west to see if a change of climate might help her condition. He warned her that he would not write to her while she was there, as "distance didn't lend

Wedding of Lewis Clarke and Florence Kenzel. *From left to right (front row)*: Stanley and Corinne; (*second row*) Dumont Jr., Lewis, Mrs. Kenzel, Florence Kenzel and William Kenzel, her brother; (*third row*) Dumont Sr., Cornelia, Alice and an unidentified groomsman. *Alice Irizarry.*

enchantment." However, when she returned, they got together again. He took her out to dinner one night to one of the fanciest restaurants in town. Rather than formally proposing, he apparently reached across the table and asked, "Florence, is it a go?" And she said, "Yes, it's a go."[97] The wedding took place in the garden at the Clarke family home, The Chestnuts, on June 12, 1901.[98]

Ernest Clarke was unable to attend the wedding. Sadly, he passed away shortly after on August 4, 1901.[99]

Alice's cousin Jessie Clarke married Phillip Raymond in Jamesport, Rhode Island, not long after Lewis's wedding. Her husband was one of the young men she had met while she and Alice were at Bordentown. He was serving as superintendent of motive power for the Quebec Southern Railway Company in Sainte Hyacinthe, Quebec, at the time. In a long, chatty letter, Jessie described the wedding and her first impressions of her new home in great detail. The sudden move to a place with a different language and culture proved a bit of a shock for her.[100]

Opp. Equitable Building   Clinton & Russell, Architects
AMERICAN EXCHANGE NATIONAL BANK, 128 Broadway.
American Exchange National Bank, cor. Cedar St. Capital, $5,000,000, surplus,
$3,700,000; assets, $51,281,975. Org'd 1839. Dumont Clarke, President.

Left: The New American Exchange National Bank building. Unidentified publication. *Author's collection.*

Opposite: The human caravan moving the bank's assets. Unidentified publication. *Louise Redfield Levy.*

While the young people were choosing their spouses, Dumont Clarke Sr. was busy dealing with the growing needs of his bank. Its business had expanded to the point where it had outgrown its current establishment and was in need of new quarters to adequately house its operations. By 1899, the original structure at 126 Broadway on the corner of Cedar Street had been torn down to make way for the new building.

During this process, the bank moved its operations to the second floor of the Boreel Building at 113 Broadway. However, that building lacked a sufficiently strong fireproof and burglarproof vault to secure the bank's large quantity of cash and securities. To safeguard these assets, the bank's officers arranged with the Mercantile Safety Deposit Company across the street to store these items in its vaults for safekeeping overnight.

At 4:10 p.m., all traffic was halted on Broadway by the policeman on the beat while the bank's security officer led a group of seven clerks chained together, each carrying two heavy strongboxes of gold and silver and followed by a dozen others with various other bank assets as they made their way across the street. Sharpshooters were stationed in the bank's windows for added security. Three of these trips were required each afternoon to get everything moved. At 4:30 p.m., the vault's time locks clicked into place. At 8:30 the following morning, the same trip was made in reverse. This procedure continued for more than a year until the new bank building was completed.[101]

Chapter 6

AN EVENTFUL FEW MONTHS

Exactly when Alice first met Henry Redfield is unclear, but she was certainly acquainted with him by the time of his brother Edwin's wedding in 1897. Over the next few years, they saw each other from time to time. Henry visited both the Worths and the Clarkes on occasion. By 1902, he, Jessie Worth and Alice were attending choral practice and other events together. Their friends began to think of them as a happy threesome. Henry began to appear fairly frequently in Alice's diary entries.

Alice had a good voice, and she took her singing quite seriously. In February 1902, she and her mother met Mme. Cappiani in New York and arranged for Alice to take singing lessons, twice a week for ten weeks.[102] She practiced her singing at home in between.

The year 1902 was a busy time for many members of the Clarke family. In mid-March, Dumont Clarke Sr. purchased his first steam yacht, the *Tranquilo*.[103] The vessel was 80 feet long with an 11.4-foot beam and had a dining saloon and three staterooms on the deck level.[104] Soon he was taking family members out for short trips on the weekends. On April 4, 1902, the *New York Commercial* published a lengthy article about him, giving a quite detailed summary of his life history and interests, his work at the bank and a list of the many companies for which he served as a director.[105]

On May 9, Dumont made his original will. In it, he left his wife, Cornelia, all his household effects, his insurance policies and a substantial sum in cash and/or securities plus all his New Jersey real estate and its improvements. The remainder of his assets was to be placed in a trust for five years, after which they were to be distributed to his children in equal shares. Lewis L. Clarke and George B. Case were to serve as trustees.[106]

Meanwhile, Stanley Clarke had been courting Juliette "Dot" Fessenden, Corinne's best friend. On April 9, they became engaged.[107] Dot was the daughter of Benjamin Fessenden, a resident of Dumont and a former sea captain, who served as superintendent of the ferries crossing the Hudson between New Jersey and New York. He also owned a commercial building in Dumont.[108]

Around the middle of May 1902, it appears that Henry Redfield said something that made Alice realize that he had a serious interest in her. Just what he said her diary doesn't reveal. She seemed not to have been aware of this before and spent a couple of days pondering the implications.[109] Previously, everyone had assumed that his interest was in Jessie Worth. After the final spring meeting of the choral group on May 22, Henry walked Alice home, and they sat on the porch and chatted. She wrote, "Henry is a great boy—Beautiful moonlight."[110]

With the birth of Mary's second child immanent, on June 9, Alice went to the Case home in New York to help out. She spent some time looking after little Mary Ermine but also continued with her singing lessons and visited friends. In the first few days, Lewis and his wife came by to visit, and Henry sent Alice a dozen beautiful red roses.[111] A few days later, he wrote her a letter. Then Mary became ill. After taking care of things for a couple of days, Alice made a quick trip home to attend Lizzie Stillman's anniversary party, where she saw Henry again.[112] Mary was still not well when she returned but feeling somewhat better. She still spent most of her time in bed.

Henry continued to be attentive to Alice. On June 24, he sent her a two-pound box of Huyler's chocolates and came to visit her at Mary's on June 29, staying for the evening. Apparently, he had determined to end his relationship with Jessie Worth. Alice wrote, "Well, it is over with. Hope it will soon come out well. Poor boy. My heart aches for him."[113]

On the evening of June 30, Mary went into labor, and early the next morning, her first son was born. They named him George Bowen Case Jr. for his father. The initial joy of the family quickly turned to grave concern as it became clear that the child was very ill. Despite the efforts of three doctors and the nurse who had been hired to care for the little one, the baby died on July 4. Alice wrote, "What a sad hard day it has been for us all. God's will be done. It is finished."[114]

No details are given as to the nature of the child's illness. However, another of Mary's sons suffered from hemophilia, a genetic condition causing a lack of sufficient clotting proteins in the blood, making any significant trauma hazardous.[115] Since the birthing process may at times involve some trauma to the child, perhaps that same condition may have been a contributing factor in his death. Alice helped prepare the infant for burial and sent messages to notify various family members of the situation. A private funeral service was held the following day with only eight people in attendance.

On July 6, Alice returned home to Dumont. Mary Ermine and her nurse Lena came with her to spend some time while Mary continued to recuperate at home. Alice wrote ten letters on George's behalf explaining the sad situation. Henry came by the following day. They played ping-pong; he gave her another box of candy and generally helped lift her spirits, at least temporarily. That July was generally a sad one for the family; everyone tended to be out of sorts at one time or another. Alice had a couple of long talks with her brother Dumont, which helped her feel a bit better. On July 20, she wrote, "Hope we can fix matters a little. <u>God help us</u>. We sadly need it. Our task is peacemakers."[116] Shortly thereafter, tensions finally began to ease.

Alice's twenty-sixth birthday came on July 23. Henry wrote her a letter and sent her a silver perfume bottle. She wrote a long letter back to him.

On August 2, Alice and her mother set out on a trip to visit the Ellery relatives in Castleton, Vermont. Henry joined them along the way, and they

Prospect House, Lake Bomoseen, Vermont. *Author's collection.*

Above: Under the trees by Prospect House. *Author's collection.*

Right: Henry in the rowboat. *John Redfield.*

Left: Alice in the rowboat. *John Redfield.*

Below: Prospect House porch. *Author's collection.*

continued on to Albany for the night. Henry and Alice took a side trip the following day to visit the Leggetts and other friends in and around Chatham, New York, then headed back to Albany. After touring the capital in the morning the next day, they all took the train to Castleton and arrived at their hotel, Prospect House on nearby Lake Bomoseen, in the late afternoon.

Cornelia was tired and soon went to bed. Alice and Henry chatted outside under the trees for a while. "We sealed our compact tonight. Yes I'm glad."[117]

The young couple spent the next few days happily, rowing on the lake, taking photos of each other and the scenery, visiting with the Baldwins, Cornelia's sister and her physician son, plus some area friends, and finally stopping by the family graveyard. Sometimes they sat on the hotel porch reading for a while. In the evenings, they danced.[118]

On August 11, they all returned to Albany. Cornelia then went back home to Dumont, while Alice and Henry stopped off to visit with the Leggetts again. On August 14, Henry returned home, while Alice stayed on to visit longer. When she finally returned on August 19, he met her at the train.[119]

Shortly after, Henry sent her some pictures from their trip and she printed up her own. She also finally had a chance to sit down with her father and have a long talk about the situation between Jessie Worth and Henry. Henry went to the bank and had a talk with her father as well. On August 24, Henry gave Alice her engagement ring, and they looked over their pictures together. Everything seemed to be going just fine.

Chapter 7

WHO WAS THAT YOUNG MAN?

Henry Wells Redfield Jr. came from a family with a somewhat unusual history. His father, Henry Wells Redfield Sr., was born on March 31, 1841. Henry Sr.'s father, Richard, was a New York banker. His mother, Frances Anne Lowerre Redfield, died a few weeks after his birth, perhaps from complications associated with the delivery. Richard apparently was unable to take care of his children after his wife's death. From a letter he wrote to his sister-in-law a couple of years later, he appears to have been in chronic ill health,[120] and he passed away in 1846.[121] The Lowerre family took in Henry and his older brother, Richard. It is unclear who raised their sister, Frances.

While Richard grew up with his grandparents' younger children, Henry Sr. was raised as an only child by Susan Jane Lowerre, his mother's younger sister, first by her alone, and later in her household after she married Robert Crowther, a butcher, and moved to Watervliet, New York.[122] By 1860, Susan Crowther had become a widow and was living in New York City. Henry Sr. was still living with her, working as a clerk.[123]

With the start of the Civil War in 1861, Henry Sr. joined the army. Because he had lost the trigger finger on his right hand, perhaps in an accident in the butcher shop, he could not fire a gun and was assigned as a stretcher bearer to the Medical Corps.[124]

By 1863, he was no longer with the military. On June 16, he married Eliza Lavinia Foster, the daughter of William Foster, an upholsterer who lived in Williamsburg, New York, the same town as his Lowerre grandparents.

Henry Wells Redfield Sr. *Robin Crawford.*

Henry and Lavinia set up house in Brooklyn along with Susan Crowther and started a family of their own. He worked in a bank, and the family took in boarders to help defray expenses.[125] By the end of 1870, the family included four children. Herbert was born in 1864, Henry Foster in 1866, Louise in 1868[126] and Richard Edwin in 1870. Henry Sr.'s occupation was listed as bookkeeper. Susan Crowther was no longer with them.

Sometime between 1870 and 1874, tragedy struck. Young Foster, as he was called by the family, was bitten by a mad dog and died of hydrophobia.[127] When another son was born on April 2, 1874, they named him Henry Wells Redfield Jr. Daisy, born in 1877, and a third daughter, Katherine, born in 1879, completed the family.[128]

At the time of Henry Jr.'s birth, the family was living in Tarrytown, New York. While there, Henry Sr. met Malachi Taylor, a member of the Plymouth Brethren and Bible teacher. Although the family had previously been Baptist in its religious persuasion, Henry Sr. embraced this different approach to religion, and soon he was hosting weekly Bible studies led by Taylor in his home. Later, when the family moved to Tenafly and then Closter, Taylor continued to visit, and they started a Brethren meeting. After Taylor died, Henry Sr. continued the meetings in his home.[129]

The Plymouth Brethren are considered to be a conservative evangelical Christian movement, an offshoot of the Church of England, composed of people who disliked the ritual and what they perceived as corruption present in that church in the early 1800s. The movement traces its origins to Dublin, Ireland, in the 1820s, although leaders of the movement later established themselves in Plymouth, England, in the 1830s where they began to develop a serious following. Members see themselves not as a denomination, but rather as a network of like-minded independent churches. Because the different meeting groups are semiautonomous, there can be a significant difference in specific practices from one group to another, such as how they refer to themselves, whether as members of either a Gospel Hall or a Chapel, and whether they regard themselves as an open or closed group with regard to membership.[130] The variations are many and beyond our scope here, so we will stick with how the group that began in Henry Sr.'s living room developed.

Like other Brethren groups, they believed the Bible was the supreme authority for church doctrine and practice. They rejected the concept of clergy, believing all Christians were ministers. Thus, no member of the group was ordained or specifically employed to function as one. Instead the local church was led by a group of elders. Only men might serve as elders or fulfill any other leadership role in the group. Elders performed many of the duties of ministers in other denominations, counselling, visiting the sick, performing baptisms, marriages, funerals and the like. They believed in adult baptism by full immersion when an individual was old enough to personally decide to follow the religious beliefs of the group.

They also believed that according to scripture, "Women should keep silence in the church." They even said that they should not pray.[131] At prayer meetings, male members of the group might speak, offering up their thoughts on religious topics or suggesting hymns which those assembled would then proceed to sing.

Although the group's meetings were first held in the Redfield living room, they later moved across the street in Closter to his neighbor and friend Harvey Wadham's home. After Henry Sr. passed away in 1904, Harvey Wadham took over the leading role in the group. He married Katherine, Henry Sr.'s youngest daughter, in 1902.

As the meeting's size grew, it moved to larger rented quarters, first in Demarest, and then in Tenafly. There they assembled in the auditorium on the upper floor of Tenafly Hall, capable of seating up to five hundred,[132]

Tenafly Hall circa 1907. An early meeting place for the congregation who later formed Grace Chapel. *Author's collection.*

although they did not need that much space. The building had been erected by a private group in 1893. In 1894, the borough rented space there since it had no offices of its own. Other occupants were the Tenafly Society, the Tenakill Outing Club and a lodge hall. There was also some retail space on the first floor.[133]

Henry Redfield Sr. worked at various bookkeeping occupations throughout his adult life, at a variety of different locations in New York, New Jersey and also briefly in Pennsylvania. In his later years, he served as an estimator for an Iron Works Company.

He was very much a family man who adored his children and missed them when he had to be away from home, as evidenced by a letter he wrote in 1880 to his daughter Louise who was twelve years old at the time. It begins, "Oh, how I would like to see you now." And later, "I want to see you and Daisy and the baby so much. Kiss Daisy and Kitty for me....Can't you write me a letter? I'm awful lonesome, and think I might like to take you and Daisy on my lap and hold you ever so long. Love ma-ma for me, and kiss all—everybody. Your lvg. [loving] Papa."[134]

Henry Wells Redfield Jr. as an infant.
Author's collection.

Henry Jr. grew up in this warm, loving family. Nothing much is known of his early life. As an adult, he was considered to be a bit shy and not particularly outgoing but a very warm person when one got to know him. He appeared dignified and firm in his opinions but at the same time even tempered and was generally liked by all those who knew him.[135] Like his father, he embraced the Plymouth Brethren movement.

Although his father had played semiprofessional baseball, Henry Jr. himself was not athletically inclined, nor did he have much of an interest in things mechanical.[136] His interests were much more in the realm of art and design.

Professionally, he had trained as an architect by earning his degree through a correspondence course and receiving his architect's license from New York State. He then worked in New York City as a draftsman and architect for a major architectural firm, Kohn & Company, dealing mostly with commercial projects such as apartment houses and hotels.[137]

All in all, his was a complementary personality to Alice's more lively and outgoing nature.

Chapter 8
A FLY IN THE OINTMENT

The happiness and excitement over Henry's proposal and presentation of a ring lasted slightly more than a week. On September 2, 1902, Alice met with her sister Mary Case.[138] While Alice did not record precisely what Mary told her, she clearly gave Alice some serious food for thought. Knowing that having children was very important to Alice, she apparently pointed out that getting pregnant or giving birth normally might not be possible for her due to her size, something Alice clearly had not previously considered. Did Mary's action stem simply from sisterly concern, or was she perhaps trying to ward off the loss of the services of a conveniently available maiden aunt—or even a bit of both?

Whatever the motivation, once aware of the potential problem, Alice wasted no time in proceeding to find out whether and how it might be dealt with. Fortunately for her, New York City was a major medical center, and it had a hospital dedicated solely to dealing with women's issues associated with pregnancy and childbirth.

The Sloan Maternity Hospital was established in 1886 thanks to a generous donation from William D. Sloan and his wife, Emily Vanderbilt Sloan, on property owned by Columbia University. Their aim was to provide free obstetrical services to the public while at the same time providing opportunities for instruction for students in the Columbia University Medical School. For the first ten years of the hospital's operation, all patients were admitted free. It was supported by an endowment and some funding provided on a per patient basis by the state legislature. However,

Sloan Hospital as it appeared between 1897 and 1911. Unidentified publication. *Author's collection.*

these funds proved inadequate to meet all expenses. In 1897, the policy was revised to allow services to be provided for "such private patients as can be accommodated" as well.[139] That same year, due to increasing demands for services, a major addition was made to the building, more than doubling the institution's size, again thanks to the Sloans. These developments had taken place under the direction of Dr. James W. McLane, then professor of obstetrics and dean of the College of Physicians and Surgeons at Columbia.[140] In 1899, Dr. McLane retired and was succeeded by Dr. Edwin B. Cragin as professor of obstetrics.[141]

Dr. Cragin earned his undergraduate degree at Yale and graduated from the College of Physicians and Surgeons in 1886. Over the next few years, he served in a variety of positions in obstetrics and gynecology at various New York hospitals. In 1890, he produced a student manual,

Essentials of Gynecology, which became a standard reference.[142] During his service at Sloan Hospital, he came to be recognized as a leading authority in obstetrics as well.

On September 10, 1902, Alice and her mother met with Dr. Cragin. After examining her, he was able to confirm that she was indeed capable of conceiving a child, but for the child to be born successfully, it would have to be delivered by cesarean section. This information was a considerable cause for concern.

Although cesarean deliveries are now considered to be generally common and low-risk procedures, such was not the case at that time. Historically, even up through the late 1800s, cesareans were rarely performed, and even then typically only after a long and unsuccessful attempt by the mother to deliver her child naturally, which had left her near or at the point of death. The focus then was primarily an attempt to save the child. Sadly, neither the mother nor the child usually survived.

In the early 1880s, a German doctor by the name of Max Sanger developed an operating procedure that greatly increased the survival rate of both mother and child. In addition to the use of anesthesia, which had been introduced a few decades earlier, his technique involved three key points: the use of antiseptics during the procedure, the use of hemostatic forceps to help control bleeding and, perhaps most importantly, the use of sutures to sew up the uterine incision and prevent uterine discharge from entering the abdominal cavity in addition to closing the wound externally. An 1886 report by Dr. W.T. Lusk of New York to the British Medical Association showed similar encouraging results from employing this procedure.[143]

Dr. Cragin used the Sanger technique in performing his cesarean sections. By the time Alice came to consult with him, he had already done the procedure successfully a number of times. With patients he knew in advance would require the surgery, the doctor performed the operations before the women went into labor so that they would be in better physical condition to withstand the procedure. However, it was still not without risk and would have been regarded at the very least as experimental by the general public.

Was she willing to take the risk? And what would Henry think of such a situation? Would he want to shy away from it? What did it mean for their future? Still, she knew he must be told, but how was she going to do it? Between September 11 and September 14, she pondered the situation and talked with Mary again a couple of times. She spent some time with Henry as well, not letting on that anything might be amiss. On September 15, she noted, "Have made up my mind, but it hurts," and "Must make the most of my decision."[144]

On September 16, she went to dinner at the Cases and "talked matters over with George." She had decided that having her trusted friend George present the problem to Henry would be better than attempting to do so herself. She saw George and Mary again on September 18 but was unable to speak with him alone. "A nod from George tells me so much, only wish I could chat with him a few minutes."[145]

On September 20, Alice received a "sweet and sad letter from Henry." He was initially blindsided and overwhelmed by the situation:

Alice, my darling, what does it all mean? I have been trying since yesterday morning to collect my thoughts. George was in then and told me what you had done. You brave, brave girl. Does it mean we are to be separated? It can not [sic]—it must not—and yet for your sake it may be best. We must talk it over ourselves, as George said, we must decide this for ourselves. I will not be able to talk about it Sunday. I must have a little more time....Please dear, don't think I love you any less for what has taken place, in fact, quite the reverse is the fact.[146]

He also sent her a box of candy. Nevertheless, on Sunday they did talk about the situation, and Henry arranged to meet with Dr. Cragin himself. On September 23, Henry wrote again to Alice, on a much more positive note:

I have been to see Dr. Cragin, and he has told me anything it was necessary for me to know, and also gave me his opinion and advice. What it was, I will tell you when we have our talk. I will tell you now, though, that I am not greatly worried—as I think any thing [sic] will come out right. The doctor was very kind and seemed greatly pleased to relieve my anxiety.... Well, darling—I suppose our troubles are not altogether over, but for the presence [sic] let us be happy in knowledge of each other's love. I am confident—of yours, and I think you have no doubts of mine. We will meet other difficulties when we have to. Did you think for a moment dear—that I would ask you to release me? I hope you knew me better. Well, good night my Princess. From your devoted Henry.[147]

Nevertheless, around this time, Alice apparently returned his ring. She needed more time to mull over the implications of the situation.

Meanwhile, preparations for Stanley's wedding to "Dot" Fessenden were underway. The wedding took place at the Fessenden home on the evening of October 8. Corinne served as a bridesmaid. About fifty people attended.[148] It was likely at about this time that Stanley's father put him in charge of managing his New Jersey properties.

For the next few weeks, Alice continued with her daily home life much as before, sewing, reading, visiting and entertaining friends, attending choral practice and the like. Henry stopped by to visit frequently or wrote her letters, which she greatly appreciated.

On November 5, she set out for another visit with the Worth relatives and friends in the South. Henry came by the ship to see her off, bearing gifts of candy and violets.[149] While she was away, they exchanged letters frequently. At the end of her first week in Petersburg, Virginia, she received a big box of violets from Henry.[150]

On November 17, she went on to Wilmington, North Carolina, and found letters from Henry waiting for her there. A box of Huyler's chocolates arrived for her two days later.[151] Letters went back and forth between the two of them almost daily. Alice took lots of photographs, including some of cotton picking. On November 30, she took communion for the first time and joined the Presbyterian Church of Wilmington. The following day, she returned to Petersburg and spent another week or so there, then on to Washington, D.C., where she spent three days sightseeing before finally returning home on December 13.

Shortly thereafter, she let Henry know that she had decided to go ahead and marry him. On December 18, the Stillmans hosted a dinner before choral practice, and Henry presented her with her ring again. The couple was now officially engaged.

Chapter 9

THE GRAND TOUR

When Alice's mother learned that the couple was indeed planning to marry, she thought it was important that Alice have a chance to see more of the world before family responsibilities tied her down. Accordingly, Cornelia arranged to take Alice on a trip to Europe with her the following summer. The wedding was then planned for early 1904.

On June 6, 1903, Alice and her mother began their Cooks Tour, boarding the steamer *Hohenzollern* at Hoboken. On board, she found several bouquets of flowers awaiting her, including a dozen roses from Henry, plus a letter from him. Numerous friends and relatives arrived to see her off. Henry came with a big box of Huyler's candy. Others brought books and a newspaper to help her pass the time onboard. Her father and her brother Dumont had planned to come by in the *Kalolah*, the new larger steam yacht Dumont Sr. had purchased a couple of weeks before,[152] after they were underway, but did not appear.[153]

On the voyage across the Atlantic, Alice was initially a bit sad to have left Henry and the others behind, a condition exacerbated by not yet knowing any of her fellow passengers, a lack of anything very interesting to her to do aboard ship[154] and the fact that she had hit her head on a bulkhead and needed stitches to close the wound.[155] She and her mother wore one of the American Beauty roses that Henry had given her each night to dinner, until they all wilted.[156]

After sailing through the Azores without stopping, they made their first landing in Gibraltar on June 15 and spent the morning touring all the

Alice on board the *Hohenzollern* en route to Europe. *John Redfield.*

sights on the rock. That evening, the ship set sail again for Naples, which they reached three days later. She was disappointed to discover that Mount Vesuvius was not erupting at the time. After a day of sightseeing in Naples, they went next to visit Pompeii, where she enjoyed walking through the ruins and collected a small piece of lava as a souvenir. She particularly liked seeing a number of the places mentioned in the novel *The Last Days of Pompeii.*

At each place they visited, she took many pictures. She also wrote numerous letters and postcards to friends and relatives—including many letters to Henry—describing what she had seen.

On June 20, they reached Rome and spent the next three days there. The group made a special visit to St. Paul's Catacombs and a Capuchin monastery, "where skulls and bones were made into figures."[157] They then toured many of the ancient historic sites in the city, including the Forum, the Colosseum, the Arch of Constantine and the Baths of Caracalla, as well as modern places of note, such as the Hall of Liberty, the Vatican and St. Peters.

Next it was on to Florence, where they saw the Uffizi Gallery and a modern painting gallery plus the cathedral and the baptistery with its famous bronze doors. After dinner, the group leader, Mr. Cabois, played the piano, while Alice and some others enjoyed an impromptu dance.

On June 27, the group arrived in Venice and spent the morning visiting the shops in St. Mark's Square, where Alice bought some fine lace. In the afternoon, they boarded gondolas and went to visit a Venetian glass factory. The following day, they toured the Doge's Palace, the Rialto, the Bridge of Sighs and St. Mark's Cathedral, feeding the pigeons along the way, and spent the afternoon and part of the evening out in gondolas on the Grand Canal.

After a brief stop in Milan to see the cathedral, they took a train through the Alps to Lucerne, Switzerland. Alice greatly enjoyed the mountain scenery. Following a side trip to the top of Mount Rigi, they went on to Schaffhausen, where she watched the "Musiccreation,"[158] a sound and light display of the local falls of the Rhine and Schaffhausen castle, which she found most impressive.

Then it was on to Heidelberg, Germany, where they visited the castle and viewed the famous Great Tun, a huge wine barrel capable of holding almost fifty-eight thousand gallons of wine,[159] though it normally stood empty, located in the castle's cellar. Next it was on to the university, where they stopped by the students' fighting hall. Wiesbaden followed with a trip through part of the Black Forest, then a voyage down the Rhine on a steamer to Cologne. The newly appointed cardinal of Cologne happened to be traveling on the same ship to take up his position there, and the Clarkes took part in the accompanying festivities.[160]

The group arrived in Paris on July 7, and the next afternoon, Alice and her mother took a carriage ride through the Champs-Elysées to the Bois de Boulogne. After a couple of days of sightseeing, they and a group of friends attended an opera, *Les Huguenots*. Her mother was not feeling well and remained in the hotel while she and her tour friends visited Versailles. On July 13, they left Paris for Dieppe, where they boarded a steamer that took them to Dover. From there, they proceeded on to London.

The following morning their tour guide, Mr. Cabois, left. The group members presented him with a tip in appreciation of his services. Alice was sorry to see him go.[161] Over the next few days, the members of the group explored London on their own. They visited many major sites, the Houses of Parliament, the British Museum, the Tate Gallery, the Tower of London and Westminster Abbey. Others they simply drove by: Hyde Park, Kensington, London Bridge and Seven Dials, to name a few.

During the trip, Alice wrote several letters to Julia Russell, an American friend of hers who had married an Irishman and was living in London. Julia

Alice's London souvenir photo.
John Redfield.

came to visit her at the hotel and later took her out to lunch and to do some shopping at the Junior Army and Navy Store.[162] Alice obviously liked what that store had to offer, as she went back there again to get some last-minute gifts for people back home.[163]

On July 18, she went in the morning with a friend to have her picture taken at a shop near Ludgate Circus. The image shows her in a mock-up of the window of a first-class railroad carriage. That afternoon, Alice and her mother boarded a train to Dover to join their ship for the journey home.

Alice found the voyage home much more pleasant than the outgoing one. Many of the friends she had made on the trip were returning home with her at the same time. She and Miss Gleason, a fellow tour member, spent quite a bit of time comparing their notes on the various places they had visited. She also learned how to play shuffleboard and competed in the ladies' tournament. In the evenings, she sometimes played cards or simply read.

When the boat docked in New York on July 27, she was met by Henry and her brother Dumont. She arrived home before dinnertime, where she was greeted by many welcoming letters. Henry came to dinner and stayed until late in the evening. Then she and Dumont talked for another hour or so.[164]

Shortly after her return, Alice mailed Mr. Cabois copies of some of the pictures she had taken and received a most charming reply. In addition to thanking her for the photos, he told her how much he had enjoyed being a courier for the American tourist group and was looking forward to possibly leading another group scheduled to visit the United States in the near future.[165]

On September 15, 1903, Dumont Clarke added a codicil to his will. He revised the terms of his trust stating it should continue during the lives of Corinne and Dumont Jr., but not more than ten years after his death. Stanley's portion of the income of the trust was to be divided into two equal shares, one for him and one for his wife, Juliette. He also added a bequest to the Newport Trust Company of $2,000 in trust, the income from which was to be used to maintain the Clarke family plot in the Newport Cemetery.[166]

Chapter 10

TYING THE KNOT

T he date chosen for the wedding of Alice Clarke and Henry Redfield Jr. was January 20, 1904. They decided to make it a simple affair for family and close friends, held in the reception room at the Clarke home in Dumont.[167] A Brethren elder, Thornton F. Turner from the Irian Cavalry Chapel in New York, was chosen to perform the ceremony.[168]

On the eve of the wedding, Henry wrote,

> *Alice dear, this is the last letter you will—as Alice Clarke—receive from me—do you realize that? I received a letter from Mr. Turner last night—a very nice little letter it was. I will bring it out tomorrow. I also received a package from him today—for—a little gift he called it.*
>
> *Aunt Kate says she and my other relatives are going to give us a surprise party tomorrow night—that we need not all be surprised if we see them all come walking in.*
>
> *Do you begin to feel nervous? I don't, but suppose I will—don't let's let it be such an awfully solemn occasion.*
>
> *The fellows have been trying to jolly me all day—but have found it did not work very well.*
>
> *In just a little while you will be Mrs. R. do you realize that? It seems to me the most improbable thing in the world.*
>
> *Well good night my darling—Yrs. Henry*[169]

The wedding took place the following evening at the Clarke home, which was profusely decorated with roses, ferns and lilies. The event was covered by the local newspaper, the *Tenafly Record*:

> *The bride, a lovely little fairy, was gowned in white panne crepe du chine trimmed with duchesse lace. She carried a shower bouquet of orchids and lillies* [sic] *of the valley, and wore as an ornament the gift of the groom, a pearl and diamond Lavaleere* [sic]. *Miss Jessie Worth was the musician of the occasion, and to the strain of the wedding march the bride entered the reception room, leaning on the arm of her father who gave her away. She was attended by her sister, Miss Corinne Clark* [sic], *as maid of honor. The groom and his best man, Mr. Dumont Clark* [sic] *Jr., awaited them in the bay window which had been transformed into a veritable floral bower. Rev. T.F. Turner, of New York, was the officiating clergyman. Only relatives and intimate friends were present. The presents were many and handsome and included two substantial checks from the bride's parents. The bride's gift to the groom was a pearl stick pin.* [170]

Their honeymoon destination was Lakewood, New Jersey, named for the lakes and pine forests nearby. The area had become a fashionable winter resort by the 1890s due to its temperature supposedly being warmer than the New York City area. [171] The *New York Herald* noted their arrival:

> *The tiniest bride that ever came to Lakewood on her honeymoon is Mrs. Henry W. Redfield Jr., of Tenafly. She is barely four feet in height, wears a No. 12 child's shoe and a No. 1 glove and when she appears by the side of her husband, who is a broad shouldered athlete, six feet two inches in height, she looks like a beautiful doll. They appear to be supremely happy, however, and do not seem to mind the stares of the people they meet.*
>
> *Mrs. Redfield was Miss Alice Coe Clark* [sic], *daughter of Mr. Dumont Clark* [sic], *President of the American Exchange National Bank, of New York. She was married to Mr. Redfield at The Chestnuts, Dumont, N.J., her father's country place, on Wednesday.* [172]

The day after the wedding, Corinne wrote the couple a nice note, telling them all that had happened after they left. The general consensus was that everything went off beautifully. The guests all had a fine time and stayed until 10:30 p.m. Henry's father took off his coat jacket and enjoyed a game of pool. Corinne was quite taken with Mr. Turner and felt the other guests

Alice in her wedding dress. *Robin Crawford.*

enjoyed his company as well. She confessed that it was his idea to tie an old shoe to Alice's suitcase just for fun. She mentioned carefully packing away the wedding dress, described a late wedding gift and forwarded a congratulatory telegram along with her letter.[173]

Alice's mother, Cornelia, wrote to her a couple of days later. She noted how quiet the house was with Alice gone and looked forward to seeing her when they returned. She added clippings to her letter, including the one from the *Tenafly Record* that described Alice as "a lovely little fairy"[174] and commented, "The reaction from the 'great event'—and the flight of the 'little fairy' is quite offensive. Tomorrow I must seek change of thought in town."[175] She despised the use of the term *fairy*, which often appeared in press accounts of the activities of professional proportional dwarves. No doubt she found the *New York Herald*'s reference to Alice as "a beautiful doll" offensive as well.

As a postscript, she noted, "Mrs. Redfield said to me now Mrs. Clarke you have given me a daughter and I have given you a son, we ought to be the best of friends. I said indeed we would be, and kissed her goodbye. I like all the Redfields so much."[176]

Henry's mother wrote to him as well. Although his father's health was fragile, he had enjoyed his game of pool and suffered no ill effects from staying up late. She closed with some sage advice: "What delightful times you and Alice will have together. Make the most of it. Youth and happiness only come once, so store your memories full. I shall not tell you how lonesome it is without you, but I have my own memories of a son who has rarely grieved me, and has always been a friend and comfort."[177]

Apparently, Jessie Worth was still carrying a torch for Henry a year and a half after he had told her of his devotion to Alice. Corinne's letter mentioned that although Jessie did not break down during the ceremony or the party afterward, when she went home to bed, she cried herself to sleep.[178] Alice's mother noted the girl's distress: "Poor Jessie was broken up next day. Stayed here and talked a blue streak to Mary—till I literally sent her home with bisque and cake for her mother."[179] For whatever reason, Jessie Worth never married. She eventually moved to Petersburg, Virginia, to live with her brother Will.[180]

Prior to the wedding, Henry had purchased a roughly four-acre plot of land at 318 Engle Street in Tenafly.[181] The property sloped up the hillside. The original white clapboard three-story house located on the hill near the back of the property was completed in 1904.[182] In her letter to Alice after the wedding, her mother mentions that Alice's father and Corinne had

Original Redfield House and property, Tenafly, New Jersey. *Nancy Carkhuff.*

gone to Tenafly to check on how things were progressing with Alice's future home, and everything seemed to be in good shape. The painters had started work.[183] It is not known precisely when the work was completed and the couple moved in.

That same spring, Dumont Clarke Sr. purchased his third, and largest, steam yacht, the *Surprise*, 127 feet long.[184] He finally had a vessel that appeared to meet all his needs and thoroughly enjoyed it.

Henry Redfield Sr.'s health continued to deteriorate. Although he was able to see the birth of his daughter Kitty Wadham's first child, Katherine, in late November, he passed away two weeks later on December 13, 1904.[185]

Henry Jr. and Alice settled happily into their new home. It is unclear whether they initially had any help in the form of a cook or a maid.

Not too long after they moved in, most likely in the fall of 1905, there was a brush fire in the woods behind their house. Afraid that their home might catch on fire as well, they tried to wet it down. Alice was pumping the water in the basement and carrying it up to Henry so that he could put it to use wherever it was most needed. In the midst of this activity, she suddenly noticed that she had started to bleed. She realized she was having an early miscarriage. Rather than being devastated by this unfortunate event, she was excited and happy to confirm that she was able to conceive a child, and although she had lost this one, there was a real possibility that she might have another.[186] She was right.

Chapter 11

DREAMS FULFILLED

July 23, 1906, was Alice's thirtieth birthday. Her mother wrote to her the day before, "My dear little girl, Thirty years old tomorrow—I cannot realize it—may you be spared many years more to brighten our lives. I wish you many happy returns of your birthday." She goes on to note, "We miss the auto—it broke to pieces—just like last time—taking your father and George to the train. Such is life—disappointing. Papa says no more auto—hundreds of dollars gone up in smoke."[187] This unfortunate mishap was quickly forgotten a few days later when Alice told her mother that she was expecting a baby, due in early spring.

Her brother Dumont had recently completed his undergraduate studies at Princeton and was taking a brief break, going off for a couple of weeks on the family yacht. From there, he wrote,

> *Just before we left on the cruise Mother spoke to me of your condition, and of her concern for you. I have been thinking much about you Alice, and praying for you. What a blessing it would be to you and Henry if you could have a good healthy baby, and come through it yourself in better health than ever. To one who has so much pent up within herself of love and hope and kindness it would be God's greatest blessing.*[188]

Alice wrote back to Dumont, reassuring him that she was feeling well and in the best of spirits.

Although the young couple's family and friends were positive and supportive of the upcoming birth, gossips in the area were quite scandalized when they saw that Alice was expecting a child. At the time of her marriage, their consensus had been, "Poor Henry, he'll never be able to have children." That quickly changed to "Henry, the beast!" This attitude did not bother the expecting couple in the least.

While Dr. Cragin had reassured both Alice and Henry as to the relative safety of the cesarean operation, it was still by no means a common procedure even for him in 1907. In a detailed article he wrote a few years later about cesareans, he indicated that between May 31, 1898, and January 1, 1913, he had performed the procedure a total of 112 times, or an average of under 10 times per year.[189]

Dr. Cragin's procedure, when he knew in advance that a cesarean delivery was required, was to admit the mother to hospital about three weeks ahead of the baby's due date[190] and to perform the operation about two weeks before then, prior to the woman going into labor. That way both mother and child were in optimal condition to withstand the surgery.[191] The mother and baby remained in hospital for about a month after delivery to be sure that there were no complications.

Facing the reality of the upcoming cesarean delivery, rather than just thinking about the possibility, must have been a sobering experience for the parents-to-be. Fortunately, Alice's pregnancy proceeded normally. When the time came for her to go to the hospital, she simply "made up her mind she would stay there and be contented and not worry."[192]

Alice entered the hospital in February 1907. There she stayed in a private patient room that resembled a hotel room of the period, more than the medically equipped hospital rooms of today. In addition to a simple ordinary cast-iron bed on wheels for the patient and a wheeled bed table, the room contained a dresser with a mirror above on one side and a wooden wardrobe with a full-length mirror front on the other. An upholstered easy chair with a chest of drawers beside it occupied one corner of the room. A simple metal chair, presumably for the use of a visitor, was also available. An Oriental-style carpet was on the floor. The room was lit by a single tall window plus a couple of small electrical side lights located over the bed and the easy chair in addition to a ceiling fixture in the center of the room.[193]

On March 1, 1907, Clarke Redfield was born. He was a normal-sized infant, twenty-one and a quarter inches tall at birth. Following Dr. Cragin's strict emphasis on antiseptic procedures, Alice wore rubber gloves when visiting him in the nursery. Oddly, someone, presumably a staff member, placed a large bow on her head, as though she were a child as well.

Alice obtained an illustrated baby book in which to note Clarke's life's milestones and to track his height in particular to determine whether he was growing at a regular rate.[194] Mother and baby returned home on March 30.[195]

In addition to tracking her new son's growth, Alice also paid close attention to the foods he ate. When it came time to introduce the child to solid foods, the hospital provided a printed schedule calling for five feedings during the day, three to four hours apart at scheduled times. Since commercial baby foods had not yet been widely developed, each meal was prepared from scratch by the family. Preparation techniques and size of servings were described in detail. The schedule contained two separate daily menus, which were to be used alternately. In addition to fresh milk, recommended foods included bread soaked in milk, strained porridge (oatmeal or cracked wheat) with cream but no sugar, a soda cracker, a slice of lightly buttered bread, a cup of meat broth (beef, chicken or mutton), a lightly boiled egg yolk with bread crumbs, a mashed baked potato moistened with meat broth and rice pudding or junket.[196]

Unfortunately, Clarke's early life proved a bit rocky. As happens with some infants, he was initially jaundiced, and in the first few months, he suffered some bouts of illness. On a visit to his grandparents at The Chestnuts on July 23, 1907, he was baptized by a minister of the Reformed Church in America.[197] Given the religious backgrounds of his parents, Alice as a Presbyterian and Henry as a member of the Plymouth Brethren, this is quite surprising. With no information available as to the reason for this action, one can only speculate that perhaps at the time he appeared to be seriously ill and the family contacted the nearest available clergyman. Fortunately, Clarke's condition improved, although he continued to suffer a series of worrisome colds.

Alice recorded her son's infant milestones in his baby book: first smile at one month; first laugh out loud, three months; starting to crawl, seven and a half months; able to stand, eight and a quarter months; building with blocks, twelve and a half months; starting to talk, twenty months.[198] Essentially normal development.

For formal baby pictures, she turned to Gertrude Sinsabaugh, a local Tenafly photographer who specialized in photographing children, although she produced some adult portraits as well.[199]

Meanwhile, Alice's younger brother Dumont was also fulfilling a dream. While at Princeton, he joined the Philadelphian Society, a YMCA group, and became very involved in their activities. When he learned of Alice's

Alice, baby Clarke and Henry Redfield. *Robin Crawford.*

pregnancy and was reassured of her well-being, he wrote telling her of his work with them.[200] As a result of his experiences, he felt called to do missionary work, and in January 1907, he applied for a passport in order to go to India with a YMCA group to serve there.[201]

While in India, Dumont was stationed in Madras. He wrote a number of letters to the family back home, particularly to his sister Corinne. She made typewritten copies of them, which she distributed to the others. In one such letter, he described the way the YMCA ministry there was set up. Work was divided into four categories: administrational, which dealt with the management of the group's facilities; educational, dealing with classes in such subjects as English, typing and shorthand for the local soldiers and students; fundraising for general operating expenses, a daily chore; and religious work, many meetings with the local Indian people and soldiers stationed nearby, also Bible classes, personnel work and association meetings. Dumont was involved in both the fundraising and religious aspects of the work.

The fundraising was all done locally and on a daily basis. Despite the varied reactions he received from those he approached, from sympathetic to hostile, he was enthusiastic about the process. "It is great work, though. Through it I have been able to look at every possible kind of business, profession and

Government service, and I've gained an impressive knowledge of human nature. We don't believe in letters, it's personal solicitation or nothing."

Dumont's religious duties including public meetings for Indians—Christians, Hindus or Muslims alike—organized "similar to the prayer meetings at home." He also led meetings with students, Bible classes and two branch associations. He particularly enjoyed this personnel work, impressed by the fact that many of those who attended the events did so at the risk of facing shunning by family and friends, and even possibly death.[202]

In a letter written on Christmas Eve 1907, he thanked the family for letters they had sent him and mentioned that a parcel they sent seemed to have gone astray, apparently a rather frequent occurrence at the time. He asked them not to worry about it, "It's the thought, not the gift that counts," and described all the local Christmas activities that were planned.[203]

In a letter titled "Diseases of Southern India," Dumont responded to family concerns about potential risks to his health. "I know that some of you at least have the idea that India is nothing more or less than a hotbed of disease. As a matter of fact there is a good deal of disease, but nothing like you imagine."[204] He went on to note that at that time the incidence of contagious diseases was low, thanks to "modern preventive measures." At the same time, he recognized that the health of many of the Indian people was less than ideal due to basic problems like malnutrition. Leprosy and elephantiasis with their associated deformities were also prevalent. He boasted, "We, Europeans and Americans, feel every bit as safe as in London or New York.—Fever is the particular fear of the white man. It is this that we take special cautions about."[205] Most likely, he was referring to malaria.

Despite Dumont's optimism, his stay in India was cut short by ill health. Nevertheless, his experience there convinced him that he enjoyed a missionary type of life.

Meanwhile, Alice's married siblings were adding to their families. Mary and George Case welcomed a second son in July 1905. He was named George B. Case Jr., the same as their son who had passed away earlier. Lewis Clarke and his wife had a daughter in September 1907, named Florence Marguerite after her mother.

Chapter 12

A TIME OF LOSS AND CHANGE

On March 15, 1908, Dumont Clarke Sr. lost his wife, Cornelia, to cerebrospinal meningitis, an infection of the membranes covering the brain and spinal cord, usually caused by bacteria that get into the bloodstream from the sinuses, ears or throat and particularly deadly when occurring in older people. Needless to say, the family was profoundly affected. She was laid to rest in the Clarke family plot in Newport, Rhode Island.[206]

A logistical problem arose when it came to dealing with her medicine collection. Apparently, she had saved every prescription or patent medicine that the family had ever bought, and there were literally whole closets full of half-empty bottles of all kinds. Since refuse collection and recycling services were unavailable at the time, they simply dug a big trench on one side of the property and buried them all there.[207]

In addition to the various standard formalities associated with her passing, Dumont Sr. needed to change his will from the earlier versions, which had left both some of his liquid assets and all his New Jersey property to Cornelia. By this time, all of his children except Corinne had established lives of their own. Thus, in a codicil added on January 29, 1909, he determined to leave all his household effects and cattle to Corinne. He also gave her the use of all his real estate and buildings in New Jersey for a period of five years following his death. For that time, the rest of his holdings remained in trust.[208] He apparently had also established a trust, whether at that time or earlier is unclear, that paid a monthly stipend to his children.[209]

Cornelia Ellery Clarke.
Robin Crawford.

In February 1909, Stanley's wife, Dot, gave birth to a healthy baby boy. They named him Dumont Clarke III. His birth was a particular cause for joy, as the couple had lost an infant earlier. However, they also learned that they either could not or should not have any more children. As a result, Dot became very protective of her son.

About that same time, Alice announced that she was expecting her second child. Henry decided that their house was no longer adequate for their growing family. Besides, he had some ideas as to how it might be altered to better meet his wife's special needs. Since he was an architect who particularly enjoyed remodeling projects, he set to work designing a new and better version of the home. While the work was in progress, the family rented another home nearby.

On September 11, 1909, Alice entered Sloan Hospital again for the birth of her second child. Young Clarke went to stay with the Wadhams, his uncle Harvey and aunt Kittie, in Closter while his mother was away.[210] John Alden Redfield was born on September 17, 1909. Named for his Mayflower ancestor, he weighed six pounds, eleven ounces and was nineteen and a half inches tall at birth. Family tradition claims that his birth represented the first-ever successful second cesarean birth with both mother and child surviving. Whether or not this is true is unclear. But given the relative rarity of the operation at the time, it is certainly a possibility.

Dumont Sr. had regained a liking for automobiles by this time and proudly drove mother and baby home from Sloan Hospital on October 13, 1909. Young John slept all during the hour-and-a-half-long trip. Apparently, his nurse at the hospital had wagered that he would do just that and won a box of Huyler's chocolates as a result.[211] Right from the start, John was a much more relaxed and easygoing child than his older brother.

Dumont Sr. mailed monthly stipend checks to his children from the trust he had established. In his October 25 letter to Alice, he asked her to be sure to let him know when the $1,000 payment covering the expenses related to John's birth would be required so he could cover that too.[212]

Despite her small size, Alice was determined to nurse her baby, and she did so for almost three months. Only then did she gradually start to wean him to a bottle, which took another month. Slowly some more solid foods were introduced as well.[213] His recommended feedings were similar to those outlined earlier for Clarke.

Alice had had a nurse to assist her at home for a time after Clarke was born,[214] but with the advent of a second child, continuous assistance became essential. Clarke was an active two-year-old and becoming too heavy for Alice to lift,[215] not to mention that the new baby took up a good deal of her time.

She chose an older lady whom she had known for many years to assist her. Kate O'Hanlon was a cousin of Lizzie Stillman's father, Archibald Worth.[216] Alice had met her when she visited the Worth relatives in Wilmington, North Carolina.[217] Kate's father had been a blockade runner during the Civil War, and the family had subsequently fallen on hard times.[218]

Alice needed assistance, and Kate needed a place to stay and something useful to do. She took on the role of a sort of live-in babysitter, helping to care for the children's physical needs, reading to them and keeping them entertained, and was treated like a member of the family, not like a nurse or a maid.[219]

Everything seemed to be going along well until about the middle of December 1909 when Dumont Sr. came down with a cold. He tried to shrug it off and kept working. The cold got worse. After about ten days, he was no longer able to go into the city to work. Four days later, on December 26, despite the best efforts of three attending physicians, he died of acute pneumonia, with his children at his bedside.[220]

John Redfield as an infant. *Alice Irizarry.*

Extensive obituaries for him appeared in major New York newspapers as well as local New Jersey ones. He was well remembered for his personal qualities as well as his many professional accomplishments. Jeanne Altschuler quotes several of these in *Dumont Heritage*: "No man could have been further removed from the accepted type of New York financier....Even Wall Street could not corrode an integrity that was spotless, or spoil a character that was modest, gentle, and lovable in all circumstances and under all conditions" (*New York World*). "In the panic of 1907 he was one of the advisors of J. Pierpont Morgan in the measures taken to restore confidence in the market. Mr. Morgan calling on him on the score of long intimacy" (*Englewood Press*). In an editorial in the *New York Evening Journal*, Arthur Brisbane wrote, "He represented well the good, useful and moral side of our commercial interests. He will be remembered by every man who ever knew him as a high-minded, kind hearted leader among the world's successful hard workers."[221] Like his wife, Dumont Sr. was buried in the Clarke family plot in Newport.

Lewis had been made vice president of the bank about 1907. With the passing of his father, he was unanimously chosen as the bank's new president.[222]

Englewood Hospital, circa 1910. *Author's collection.*

The family made a memorial donation of $5,000 to the North Church in Dumont when it embarked on a program to expand its facilities in 1912. Alice added an additional $1,200 donation to the project.[223] Corinne decided to fund the construction of an infectious disease ward at the Englewood Hospital, the major medical facility in the area, since both her parents had died of infectious diseases.[224]

Losing both parents within a relatively short time placed a considerable strain on all concerned and appears to have brought matters to a head in a simmering dispute between Alice and her sister Mary. Angry words were uttered, and resentment festered. The precise nature of the disagreement is unknown, but apparently Alice unburdened herself to her brother Dumont, who replied in a calming manner. He pointed out that the underlying cause of the problem was not the immediate issue, but rather that it lay in their childhood relationships. Mary had been her father's favorite, and her views tended to be always deferred to, while Alice had always needed to fight for recognition of hers. As a result, Alice tended to be considered as "too independent." He noted that there were valid points on both sides but deliberately refused to go into detail, which might sidetrack the point he wished to make.

He cautioned Alice about her desire for self-justification, noting that it could be off-putting even for those who were sympathetic listeners. To her assertion that she "won't be walked upon," he replied,

You are in no danger of being walked upon. You've got the "goods" in your character, your demonstrated courage, ability etc. Since you so clearly have them, you can fight your battle best by simply being yourself and not saying much about your positions, one way or the other. Dignity! Why your dignity is in yourself. You can afford to humble yourself many times—yes down to the dust!

He went on to apologize for the criticism, but it was "because I love you, and because I dare say what love thinks." He acknowledged that he believed that in the main she was right but urged her to have a forgiving attitude. He then exhorted her to make up her mind that she would "love Mary as never before" and that she should "go to see her and tell her that you have judged hastily." Then he commented wryly, "Ah, that's a lot, I know it."[225] Alice appeared to take his message to heart, carefully preserving the letter. However, the Redfield and Case families were never particularly close afterward.

Not long thereafter, Dumont completed his training at the Princeton Theological Seminary. He was ordained a Presbyterian minister and moved to Chicago, where he served with the Reverend Dr. J.GK. McClure. He met Dr. McClure's daughter Annie, and the couple married on June 20, 1911.[226] Annie's brother, J.G.K. McClure Jr., known as Jim, took part in the wedding as well, and the two soon became fast friends. The newlyweds moved to Manchester, Vermont, where they built their new home with Jim's help in the spring of 1912.[227]

Stanley continued to manage the Clarke family holdings in New Jersey. Lewis and his wife had a second daughter, Lois, in 1912. That same year, Mary Case gave birth to a third son, Robert D. Case. Sadly, they soon discovered that Robert suffered from hemophilia and had to be constantly protected from the slightest injury.

At first, Corinne had her aunt Sarah Ellery come and live with her in the family home. However, they did not get along with each other well.[228] She realized that her time staying there was limited by the terms of her father's will and decided to build a house of her own in nearby Demarest, New Jersey. When Corinne moved to the new location, she went by herself and took the greenhouse with her.[229]

Chapter 13

REMODELING THE FAMILY HOME

For a number of years, Henry Redfield had worked for the architectural firm of Kohn and Company in New York as an architect and draftsman doing large commercial projects like apartment buildings and hotels. He then decided he preferred to work on smaller projects and went into partnership with Henry Wilkinson of Llewellyn Park, New Jersey, designing and remodeling houses. He particularly enjoyed the challenge of renovations. After planning out the process and starting the work, one frequently came across unexpected complications, like beams running the wrong way, and had to figure out how to work around such problems.[230] One of his early efforts was redesigning and reconstructing his home in Tenafly to better accommodate his wife's needs and his growing family.

Henry's new design for the home required major alterations, as well as the enlargement of the structure to two or three times its original size. While the work was in progress, the family needed a different place to live. They decided to move to a small home nearby,[231] located just behind an older home built in 1873 only two doors down the street from the Redfield property. The Wadhams had purchased that older home in 1910.[232]

Henry hired a local carpenter, Christie Westerville, to do the work. When offered the job, Westerville originally demurred, pointing out that previously he had always worked under someone. However, Henry insisted, "Well, you can do it, and I want you to do it." Westerville eventually agreed. He ended up overseeing all the work, except the construction of the front staircase,

The original house with windows removed at the start of renovations. *John Redfield.*

The renovated house from a slightly different angle. *Alice Irizarry.*

which unfortunately had steps that squeaked. He vowed that never would have happened if he had been responsible for building it.[233]

A number of the home's features were specifically designed for Alice's benefit. The laundry room was located on the first floor, rather than in the basement, as was customary at the time. The two big laundry tubs had stools underneath, so Alice could climb up to use them if she had to. A gas jet was installed low to serve a two-burner stove, intended to heat a copper boiler for use in boiling clothes, a common practice. It also came in handy for heating the copper kettles used in canning the fruits and vegetables the family grew on the property. Another special feature was a ground-floor lavatory, in addition to the bathroom on the second floor, again unusual for that time. All so Alice would not need to run up and down stairs. She did that anyway.

Henry also included a feature reflecting his own interests in Japanese-style architecture. He placed large picture windows in the west wall of the living room looking down the hill toward Engle Street, providing an airy, roomy effect. At the time, no other house in Tenafly had such windows. Alice was rather embarrassed by them, feeling that they were too showy, and promptly had curtains made to cover them. However, the curtains were pushed aside every day.[234]

The second floor of the home had additional special features. A small kitchenette contained a sink and a hotplate for heating bottles of baby formula.[235] A room, intended originally as a drafting room for Henry, proved to be inadequate for that purpose, and soon developed into an office for Alice, while his drafting area moved to the third floor.[236] Another small room with a fireplace in the corner served as a cozy library. A large master bedroom was located above the living room and an enclosed sunporch containing a couch added off to the side. Alice washed her stockings and her husband's socks in the bathroom basin every day, and she could hang them out to dry on the porch regardless of the weather.[237] Two additional bedrooms on the second floor were initially occupied by the two boys. All the sinks and doorknobs in the house were set low so Alice could easily reach them.[238]

A major portion of the third floor was designed as a playroom for the children. It had a specially installed cork floor to reduce the noise from their activities to help keep it from bothering the people below. The area also included a stage that rose about eight inches off the floor and covered an area about seven feet long by about four feet deep. On the back wall behind it was a door to a portion of the attic that served as a dressing room. That room also provided access to the rest of the attic, so one could leave the stage through the door and sneak around behind the audience and surprise them.[239]

A dumbwaiter went from the third-floor playroom down to the laundry room. Although intended primarily for sending laundry down to be washed, it could also be used to send snacks requested by the children up to the playroom or to call up to notify them of callers.

For more conventional communications at the time, the house was also equipped with speaking tubes, which went from the kitchen to the upstairs sitting room. The tubes had covers with a small hole in them. To attract the attention of someone at the other end, one blew through the hole, making a whistling sound, then proceeded to give the message.[240] In addition to all the structural features, "crickets," low stools on which Alice could rest her feet when she chose to sit, were scattered throughout the house.

The house itself was situated near the upper end of the southeast corner of the property. A long, curving driveway rose up to the house from Engle Street. Beside the house to the north was a flower garden. Henry was fond

The driveway under construction. *Nancy Carkhuff.*

of flowers and knowledgeable about gardening. One of his particular efforts along that line was planting a large bed of iris, seventy-seven different types, next to the house.[241] Beyond the gardens to the north was a small orchard. Below the gardens and the orchard, and screened by a row of lilacs, was the vegetable garden. The work on the house was completed in 1912, and the family moved back in.

Chapter 14

THE BOYS' EARLY LIFE

From the time they were young, Clarke and John led varied and active lives. For Clarke's second birthday, he had his first party with his cousin Katherine Wadham and the Stillman children attending. At age three, he got to ride on his Uncle Dumont's pony.[242] His particular pride and joy, however, was his pedal car, which he drove on the walk beside the house.

Unfortunately, it became apparent quite early that John had a tendency to be a bit cross-eyed. By age three and a half, he started having drops put in his eyes regularly. He also wore glasses to try to correct the condition. They did not seem to bother him particularly.[243]

The family went on vacations each summer either to the seashore at East Quogue on Long Island or to Queechy Lake near Canaan, New York. The summer of 1911, they spent time at both places. John was not quite two years old, and he caused considerable excitement by falling out of a boat at Queechy Lake. Fortunately, the water where he did so was only a foot deep. No harm done.

Clarke particularly liked rowing at Queechy Lake. By the time he was four and a half years old he could row a large boat with two people in it by himself.[244]

At home in the spring or fall, the boys might go off exploring along the brook in the woods behind the house with Katherine Wadham and the Stillman children, taking a picnic lunch along. While the other children typically brought sandwiches to eat, Clarke and John always came with a full meal: meat, potatoes and a vegetable. Due to their mother's short

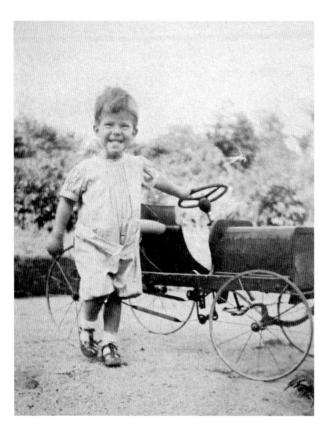

Left: Clarke and his pedal car. *Nancy Carkhuff*.

Below: Clarke and Alice rowing at Queechy Lake. *Nancy Carkhuff*.

Henry and John at Queechy Lake with Katherine Wadham, inserted in John Redfield's baby book. *Louise Redfield Levy*.

John at the seashore at East Quogue 1913. *John Redfield*.

stature, their parents carefully monitored their growth and made a point of watching their diet to ensure they always had plenty of good nutritious food to help them grow.[245]

There was a large stump of a dead chestnut tree with many trunks between the Stillman and Redfield properties, and the children often used that as a sort of playhouse. One of the trunks had a hole in it, and from time to time, Clarke and Katherine Stillman, who were good friends, used to leave messages there for each other. Katherine was careful never to start a note with the words, "Dear Clarke," for fear that if someone else found it she would get teased.[246]

When there was a good snowfall in the winter, the boys would go sledding down the hill in front of the house. The neighborhood children frequently joined them.

The Redfield and Wadham families got together on holidays when the children were young. For Thanksgiving, along with the children's grandmother Lavinia and aunts Louise and Daisy, they gathered for dinner at the Redfields'. Back then, the area usually saw snow on Thanksgiving. Katherine Wadham remembered going coasting down the front lawn afterward, sliding all the way down the hill across Engle Street and up the neighbor's driveway. On Christmas, the families opened their presents at home and gathered later at the Wadhams' for dinner.[247]

Alice had a knack for being able to relate to children without talking down to them. She could fit herself to any child's age. While she might talk nonsense with an infant, she never talked over the head of an older child. Katherine Wadham noted, "I never remember Aunt Alice ever talking over my head; and yet I can never remember her treating me like a child particularly. And when I was older I used to run over and sit and visit with her once in a while. And we would talk about all kinds of things. She always made you feel as if you were the person that she just wanted to see at that moment."[248] When Katherine had grown to about her size, Alice gave her two or three of her old house dresses. Katherine was thrilled to be able to dress up just like an adult.[249]

Discipline in the Redfield family was relatively strict but fair. The parents presented a united front. Alice was the primary disciplinarian, but whichever parent was in charge at the time was backed up by the other. Given her small size, Alice knew she needed to always be in control. As John described the situation, since she could not physically enforce a no, she had to control a situation by force of personality. If a child wanted to do something she did not approve of, she would not say, "You can't do it," but "I don't want you

Clarke and John on a sled, 1912. *Tenafly Public Library.*

to" or "I'd rather you didn't." And that was the law. There was essentially always a valid reason for that prohibition.[250]

Inappropriate behavior was not tolerated. At Clarke's sixth birthday party, after the children had their ice cream and cake, Clarke deliberately lifted up his plate and licked it with his tongue. He was promptly sent up to his room and forced to miss the rest of the fun and games.[251]

Later on, a striking example of the effectiveness of her approach occurred when Clarke, who at the time in question had grown much bigger than Alice, did something very bad for which she felt he needed to be punished. She told him to lie down on the bed so she could spank him, and he did it.[252]

At the same time, Alice was not one to hover or act overly protective. The children liked to run around on the Redfield's low garage roof. When a neighbor came by and asked if Alice was worried by them being up there, she replied, "Oh no, I just trust the Lord and let them go."[253]

Stanley's son Dumont, on the other hand, tended to suffer from overprotective parenting. His mother had lost a son in infancy earlier and been either unable to or advised not to have any more children after Dumont was born.[254] Everywhere Dumont went up until the time he was about eight years old he was accompanied by a nurse in a starched white uniform, and his activities were frequently restricted due to fears he might suffer from such ills as "overheating."[255] The Redfield children and their friends considered him a bit of a sissy as a result. When he did visit the Redfields, he usually ended up getting into a fight with Clarke.[256]

Formal education was a priority for the Redfields. Whether from concern regarding the quality of education available in the overcrowded Tenafly Public School, or perhaps because they had been brought up in a similar manner or even a bit of both, the Redfields, Stillmans and Wadhams got together and decided to hire a teacher of their own to work with their children. Miss B.K. Detriville had previously served as both a governess and a teacher in the local schools, so she seemed well qualified for the position.[257]

Initially, this mini school met at the Wadham home. Clarke had begun classes there by the time he was four years old, and John, although only two, went along at times, as he enjoyed the singing. With the completion of the Redfield home renovation in 1912, semester closing exercises were conducted on the third-floor stage there. The children recited short passages and sang songs they had learned for an audience of parents and relatives. Classes moved to the Redfield home in 1915.[258]

Unfortunately, Miss Detriville proved less than ideal for her position at times. She apparently failed to learn from the parents some of the important terminology the young children used to express their needs. When Clarke told her, "I want to make a puddle!" she did not realize that he was trying to explain that he needed to use the restroom and told him to get back to work. Little Katherine Wadham finally had to tell her what the problem was.[259]

She also had her own idiosyncratic ideas about some things, such as how certain words should be pronounced. She insisted that the word *soldier* should be pronounced "sole-dee-yer," much to Clarke's exasperation.

The Wadham family in their association with Grace Chapel had hosted a missionary who had returned from spending some time in India. Katherine was intrigued by his description of the Himalayas. But when she tried to tell Miss Detriville about it, the lady insisted on referring to the mountains as "Him-a-lay-az," and would not accept "Him-ol-yaz" despite the fact that the man who had actually been there referred to them that way.[260]

By the time they were ready for fifth grade, the children went on to the regular Tenafly School.[261] Their reactions to their homeschooling experience were varied. Katherine Stillman thought that on the whole Miss Detriville had got them off to a pretty good start.[262] However, Katherine Wadham felt that the preparation she had received was less than ideal.[263] John did not comment on the quality of the experience one way or the other.

While the children's reactions to Miss Detriville were varied, they all thoroughly adored Alice and came to her defense in any situation where they felt she was slighted. Clarke was walking up the hill on his way home from school with another boy one day, and they saw Alice coming down the hill toward them. "Who is that funny little woman?" the boy asked. "That's my mother!" Clarke responded, and he ran over and gave her a big kiss.[264]

Religion also played a prominent role in Redfield family life, as it did in the Wadham family as well. After her marriage, Alice attended the Plymouth Brethren meetings with her husband, and when the children came along, they did also. By this time, the meetings were held in Washington Hall, located on Washington Street in downtown Tenafly. The Sunday morning service was dedicated to the Lord's Supper, with the congregation sitting around a table where bread and grape juice were displayed. The men in the group would speak as they felt moved to do so. One might also suggest an appropriate hymn after a speaker finished his comments. The singing was started by another male member of the group. These meetings varied in length, usually from about an hour to an hour and a half. In the early afternoon, Sunday school met for an hour, and in the late afternoon, there was another church service.[265]

However, this peaceful, orderly lifestyle was destined to change significantly when the United States entered the First World War.

Chapter 15

WARTIME AND CAMP MERRITT

T he assassination of Archduke Franz Ferdinand of Austria in Sarajevo, Bosnia, on June 28, 1914, initiated what soon became a major international conflict and developed into World War I. The United States adopted a policy of neutrality. Public opinion in general at that time favored staying out of the war. Besides, the country's military and naval forces were small and not well prepared for serious conflict in addition to lacking experience in recently developed military tactics, such as trench warfare and aerial attacks. However, at the same time, the country was making loans to Britain and its allies, which used the money to purchase war materials from American companies.[266] While there was concern regarding the conflict, everyday activities for most people initially were not greatly affected.

The five-year trust that had been established at the death of Dumont Clarke Sr. came to an end in December 1914. His son Dumont Clarke, a pacifist like most Protestant clergy at that time, found that he owned some stock in a company that manufactured submarines and that it was increasing rapidly in value. Not wanting to profit from the war, he sold it off.[267]

After a brief visit to the seaside at East Quogue in June 1914, the Redfield family decided to try a new location for their summer lake vacation. They spent two weeks in the town of Summit, New York, staying at the Crowes Nest, a resort on Summit Lake with its own private beach.[268] They returned there again in the summer of 1915 but stayed home in 1916 due to a polio scare.

On May 1, 1915, Alice gave birth to a daughter. She weighed six pounds, twelve and a half ounces on arrival.[269] Her parents were delighted to have a girl. While John's birth as a second successful cesarean had been noteworthy, this child's birth five and a half years later was hardly considered remarkable, as cesarean delivery had become much more common by that time. They named the girl Louise for Henry's eldest sister, who was delighted by the honor. She wrote, "I think it is perfectly lovely of you and Henry to name the baby for me. I am walking with my nose way up in the air this morning."[270]

In December 1916, Alice and the two boys joined the Burroughs Nature Club, and each received an attractive illustrated certificate attesting to that fact.[271]

During the first two weeks of July 1917, the family once again vacationed at Summit Lake.[272] Shortly after her return to Tenafly, Alice entered Sloan Hospital, where her youngest son, Frank Ellery Redfield, was born on July 23, completing the family.[273] He was named for his maternal great-grandfather. Following the births of the younger children, Clarke and John moved their rooms up to the third floor.

Meanwhile, a scant week after Louise's birth, a British passenger liner the *Lusitania*—with 128 U.S. citizens on board—was sunk by a German U-boat. President Woodrow Wilson demanded that Germany stop attacking passenger ships, and Germany agreed to do so. Both former president Theodore Roosevelt and various British delegations urged President Wilson to take a more active role in the conflict, and he realized that doing so would be necessary if he was going to have some say in the peace negotiations when they eventually came. Various attempts were made to enhance preparedness in the army and navy but were essentially thwarted by the opposition to the war.

Then the Germans decided to resume unrestricted submarine attacks on shipping, knowing this action would cause war with the United States but figuring the country was too weak to effectively retaliate before the war would be over anyway. Seven U.S. merchant ships were torpedoed and sunk. The Germans also sent a telegram—intercepted and decoded by the British—to the Mexican government, urging them to attack to regain the territories of Texas, Arizona and New Mexico. Congress voted to declare war on Germany on April 6, 1917.[274]

It soon became clear that Germany had severely underestimated both the resolve and the resources of the country. Within six months, the army rose from 120,000 regulars to 1,300,000. The number of officers went from 12,000 to almost 60,000. The navy increased from 64,680 to 250,000

John, Alice and baby Louise.
Alice Irizarry.

and the marines from 13,266 to 32,000. The number of ships tripled, with more under construction. The quartermaster corps expanded from 5,000 to 50,000. The medical corps grew from 6,600 to 70,000. Draft registration was instituted, and 687,000 draftees were sent to training camps. The country's railroads were coordinated into a single continental system, and numerous other changes were made.[275]

The effect on northeastern New Jersey was immediate and profound. During the Mexican Expedition against Pancho Villa in 1915, the area had been chosen as a potential site for an embarkation camp, although it had never been used. A large, relatively sparsely settled, essentially agricultural plateau sloping gently from north to south with railroad service on both sides located a short distance from the embarkation port of Hoboken could fairly easily be developed to meet the military's needs.[276] But first, construction had to take place.

The area designated for the camp included most of the borough of Dumont plus portions of Cresskill to the east and Bergenfield to the south and comprised a total of about 770 acres covering an area about a mile long and three-fourths of a mile wide when completed. Of that acreage, 580 acres were used to provide accommodations for the soldiers, while the remaining 190 acres were used for warehouses, railway areas, an athletic field and a 60-acre truck garden to grow some of the vegetables needed to feed the men.[277] The territory occupied by the camp was either rented from the current owners or purchased outright. The camp was named in honor of Major General Wesley Merritt (1836–1910), who had served notably in the Civil War and later commanded the Philippine Expedition during the Spanish-American War, capturing Manila in 1898.[278] His wife donated $10,000 for the construction of a soldiers' club at the camp named Merritt Hall in his memory.[279]

The camp's construction crew set up headquarters in what had formerly been the Clarke family home at the corner of Madison and Chestnut Streets in the summer of 1917.[280] One of the first structures built, intended as officers' quarters, was next to the house and was pressed into service while still under construction to provide a fifteen-bed hospital and residence space for the first twenty army medical personnel to arrive. Initially, this hospital dealt primarily with accident victims and sent occasional overflow patients to the Red Cross Hospital in Cresskill.

The regular soldiers camped out in tents in a field nearby, waiting for the construction of barracks for them to be completed. In a light-hearted moment, as yet unaware of the realities of war, they might strike impressive poses for photos to be sent back home.

By November 1917, large numbers of troops were being processed through the camp. As might be predicted with many individuals living in close quarters, outbreaks of measles, mumps, scarlet fever and other infectious diseases occurred, more than the camp's facilities could handle at the time. Two wards of Englewood Hospital were taken over temporarily to deal with the overflow, and nursing staff at the hospital voluntarily gave up their rooms in one of the wings and moved in with local families, freeing up twenty-two additional beds.[281]

Initially, there were only dirt roads serving the area, so transportation in bad weather could be a challenge. No ready access to banking facilities was available locally, and the workmen experienced difficulty in trying to cash their paychecks.

Stanley Clarke came up with a solution. With his family banking connections, he could easily acquire appropriate amounts of cash. On payday, he would load a suitcase with money and drive up to the camp with

Soldiers in fierce poses outside their tent, Camp Merritt, New Jersey, October 10, 1917. *Author's collection.*

his young son Dumont. There he would roll down the back window of the car and cash the paychecks for the workmen. Dumont counted out the cash for him. He charged ten cents for each check cashed and used the funds to help provide entertainment equipment for the Hostess House where his wife volunteered, serving visitors to the camp who came to see their soldier relatives. The funds also helped purchase useful equipment for the base hospital.[282] Later, the camp's post exchange and service organizations took over the financial duties.

The first phase of construction of the base hospital was completed and opened for use on January 9, 1918. It was staffed by 20 medical officers, 11 nurses and 97 enlisted men and had a capacity of 416 beds. By November 1, 1918, its services had expanded to include 90 medical officers, 300 nurses and 605 enlisted men, and its capacity had risen to 2,500 beds.[283] It occupied the majority of the former Clarke estate and some adjacent areas as well. During the Spanish flu epidemic in the fall of 1918, bed capacity expanded to 3,800. After the armistice, capacity was expanded further to 5,400 for the debarkation period.[284]

When completed, the camp had a capacity of 2,000 officers and 40,000 enlisted men. The maximum number required to operate the camp at the time of the armistice was approximately 500 officers and 7,000 enlisted men.[285] The rest were transient, initially on the way to overseas postings and, at the war's conclusion, passing through in the process of returning home. In all, 1,088,081 soldiers moved through Camp Merritt, a little more than half on their way overseas and a slightly smaller number on their way home. Most of those in transit stayed there only three to four days.[286]

Knowing that the men, many of whom were farm boys from rural areas, would find the temptation to visit the city of New York irresistible, the transients were usually granted, half of a unit at a time, twenty-four-hour passes so that they could go see the sights.[287] However, there was a well-known hole under the camp's perimeter fence where soldiers might sneak out if they didn't have a pass.[288]

The camp became essentially a small city, with 14.3 miles of concrete road, 4.0 miles of railroad spur from the North Shore Railway in Dumont to the warehouses, water and sewer facilities, electric lighting in the buildings and streetlamps along the streets.[289] It even had its own powerhouses.

Merritt Hall, located in the center of the camp, was a large, long, low structure with 20,100 feet of floor space. It opened on January 30, 1918. A portion of the front lobby was set aside as an area for soldiers to relax and read, furnished with wicker chairs and tables, reading lamps and a large homey fireplace, topped with the altruistic motto, "We Go To War Against War." Across the lobby were the chaplain's office and the information desk, where soldiers could obtain writing materials, stamps and informational pamphlets. Next came the library room, operated by the American Library Association and containing over twenty thousand volumes. With about two dozen tables and hundreds of chairs, it could accommodate two or three hundred men at a time. A restroom with a woman attendant was provided

A pass for a member of a transient military unit. *Author's collection.*

Soldiers relaxing in the Merritt Hall lobby. *Author's collection.*

for wives and sweethearts who came to visit. A large cafeteria provided just about anything from soda fountain beverages and snacks to full course meals. Finally, there was the game room, with billiard tables, Victrolas and pianos for other entertainment.[290]

Other camp facilities consisted of a dental infirmary; a barbershop; post exchanges, at least one of which included a shoe store;[291] tailor shops; a bakery; and a refrigeration plant for perishable foods like meats and dairy products. A school for bakers and cooks supervised 164 kitchens throughout the camp. Three fire stations equipped with the latest firefighting equipment stood ready to deal with any conflagration.

An insurance department and a department selling liberty bonds were also provided.[292] A salvage department repaired and returned for reissue large numbers of pairs of shoes and items of clothing. It also dealt with the disposal of junk and waste materials.[293] The camp post office sent and received millions of letters and issued over $1.5 million worth of money orders. The Western Union office sent and received an average of 100,000 telegrams a week and made transfers of $3 million during its existence. Express and telephone services were also available.[294]

The Red Cross provided personal services to the patients in the hospital. These included comfort kits of small articles and property bags, plus games, writing paper and delicacies like fruits and jams. The organization also

The YWCA Hostess House by the camp's main gate on Knickerbocker Road. *Author's collection.*

operated a convalescent house for patients not needing medical care but not yet fit to return to work, providing them with books, musical instruments, a billiard table and other light amusements, plus regular entertainments four times a week. The Red Cross Visitor House in Tenafly gave family and friends a place to stay.

The YMCA operated seven units in the camp; the largest could serve three thousand people at a time. For the soldiers headed abroad, it provided instruction in French. For the soldiers returning, it offered a broad spectrum of vocational training courses: accounting, agricultural practices, auto mechanics, typewriting, tailoring and telegraphy being just a few examples. Religious meetings and Bible classes were also available.

The YWCA operated three Hostess Houses at the camp, providing a place where soldiers could meet with their relatives who came to visit. The National Catholic War Council also operated a small Hostess House.

The Knights of Columbus had three buildings on site and presented some form of entertainment every night. The members advertised "Everybody welcome, everything free" and provided a variety of snacks, small necessities and sports equipment for those who came by. Boxing matches, movies and vaudeville acts were among the entertainments offered. The Knights also held weekly dances, bringing in two hundred girls to partner the men. The Jewish Welfare Board provided religious services and kosher meals for members

A group assembled for a Knights of Columbus movie night. *Author's collection.*

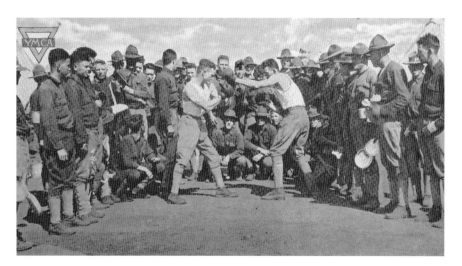

A YMCA-sponsored boxing match. *Author's collection.*

of that faith. Like the other service groups, it also offered entertainment, educational activities and free supplies and refreshments.[295]

The country's entrance into the war had a significant effect on a variety of local business operations. Henry Redfield and his partner Henry Wilkinson found that people were not very interested in building and renovating houses during that time. They suspended their architectural business and went to work for the American Red Cross.[296] Henry Redfield assumed the position of associate field director for the Red Cross at the USA Embarkation Hospital in Hoboken, New Jersey.[297] Wounded soldiers from overseas were brought there and treated until they were sufficiently recovered to continue on to their next destination.

Henry's work consisted of helping the men to reestablish their connections with family members and make any other necessary contacts. Periodically, he would arrange for busloads of them to come out to his place in Tenafly for parties. While some were content to sit back and enjoy their visit to the country, others retired to the garage to shoot craps. Even though he knew that was going to happen, it still annoyed Henry whenever it occurred, as it went against his religious beliefs.[298]

One of the soldiers Henry was working with in Hoboken was from New York City. While the man was in hospital in Hoboken, his young son happened to require hospitalization in the city. The family lived in a busy, noisy part of town next to the elevated railway where trains were constantly coming and going. When the child was ready to return home, Henry thought it would aid the boy's recovery to spend some time at his own home in Tenafly, with peace and quiet and fresh country air. The poor child woke up screaming the first night he was there. He could not stand being in such a quiet place compared to what he was accustomed and returned to his downtown home the following day.[299]

Meanwhile, Stanley Clarke was elected mayor of Tenafly, a longtime goal of his. He took office on January 1, 1918. He had worked his way up through the ranks, serving in a variety of positions: clerk to the board of election, assistant postmaster, overseer of the poor, district clerk of the school board, assessor, freeholder and councilman before finally gaining the position.

At his first council meeting, in addition to obtaining approval for the budget and appointing various town officials, he spent a significant amount of time dealing with issues regarding taxi service. With Camp Merritt close by and numerous visitors arriving to see their loved ones there, many local residents were eager to obtain taxi licenses in order to assist them. At the same time, there were also problems with some of those already holding licenses, complaints of reckless driving, driving drunk and refusing to take customers to their residences.[300]

At this time, Fiorello La Guardia, who later became mayor of New York, was serving as the liaison officer for Camp Merritt at the Tenafly Station where both the train and the trolley from New York stopped. Liaison officers were placed at each of the local stations to direct incoming troops to the

Right: Stanley Clarke, mayor of Tenafly. *Tenafly Public Library.*

Below: Tenafly Station and Trolley. *Author's collection.*

camp.[301] When the men arrived, he and Stanley Clarke would march with them up Knickerbocker Road the mile and a half to the camp.

Years later, when Louise and her husband went on a road trip out west and stopped at gas stations to fill up their car, the attendants often asked them where they were from. When they responded, "Tenafly," they frequently heard, "Tenafly, New Jersey! That's where I got off the trolley and two funny little men met us and marched us up to Camp Merritt." At five feet, two inches, La Guardia was short, although not nearly as short as Stanley at four feet, one inch. When Louise explained who LaGuardia was and told them that Stanley was her uncle, they would then reminisce about their time at Camp Merritt and might even forget to ask for payment for the gas.[302]

Tragedy struck the Case family during the war years. Young George Case Jr. suffered a ruptured appendix as a result of a football injury. Whether medical intervention could have saved him was questionable, but his mother, Mary, was a firm believer in Christian Science and refused to get him medical treatment. He died as a result.[303]

With the cessation of military hostilities on November 11, 1918, people's lives began to slowly return to normal. But it was a new normal, not simply a return to the way things had been before.

Chapter 16

READJUSTING

With the armistice on November 11, 1918, everyone breathed a sigh of relief, but things could not change immediately. Bringing the soldiers back from Europe and getting them ready to reenter civilian life had to be done in stages. Those with injuries that were not healed required additional medical care before they could leave for home. Camp Merritt continued in operation until 1920. Then the rented properties were returned to their owners, the railroad spurs were removed and the surplus contents of the warehouses were sold off. A number of fires contributed to the destruction of the camp's buildings.[304]

On Decoration Day, May 30, 1924, a monument to the camp, located at the intersection of Madison Street and Knickerbocker Road was dedicated by General John J. Pershing. In the form of an obelisk, it was engraved with the names of all 563 individuals—558 enlisted men, 4 army nurses and 1 civilian—who died while serving at the camp.[305] Stanley Clarke served on the Honorary Committee of the Camp Merritt Memorial Association, which was responsible for its construction.[306]

Stanley completed his second term as mayor of Tenafly on December 31, 1921. He joined the Sweets Company of America, the manufacturer of Tootsie Rolls, in New York. His brother Lewis served as a member of the board of directors, and Stanley served as vice-president.[307]

He and Fiorello La Guardia remained good friends. When Stanley went to work for the Sweets Company, which was located near the New York Public Library, La Guardia arranged for him to have a parking space in the library lot so he could walk to work.[308]

Camp Merritt Memorial from the booklet prepared for the memorial dedication, May 30, 1924. *Author's collection.*

After their Red Cross work at the Hoboken Hospital was completed, Henry Redfield and his partner Henry Wilkinson reestablished their architectural office in New York. However, with the onset of a recession in the early 1920s, they moved their offices to Wilkinson's home in Llewellyn Park, New Jersey. Henry Redfield worked there four days a week and also worked at home, using his drafting table up in the third-floor playroom area. He continued to enjoy working on home renovation projects because of the challenges they presented, often necessitating changes in their original plans. In addition to projects in the New Jersey area, they also accepted jobs in Pennsylvania and New York.[309]

When he was finalizing plans for a project, Henry would bring them to Alice and ask her opinion on what he proposed. Alice, who knew how to read plans but not very well, would tell him, "Henry, those are fine." He would respond, "That's what you always say. Can't you find something wrong?" She finally discovered that he usually forgot a linen closet, so that was what she first looked for on the plan. When she pointed this out to him, he happily put the closet in.[310]

One of the firm's wealthy female clients in Llewellyn Park was so pleased with the work that the architects had done on her home that she begged Henry to do the landscape gardening for her as well. He explained that he was not really an authority on that but finally agreed to do the job. It soon became apparent that the lady was attracted to him and making excuses to keep him around. So Henry invited Alice to go with him to the job one day and took her all through the house and around the gardens. It was clear to anyone who saw them together how close they were. He had no further problems with the client after that.[311]

Henry served on the Tenafly School Board for many years in the 1920s. When the board decided to build its own high school, it received a special dispensation from the state allowing it to act as its own contractor, due to the fact that Henry was an architect and his friend and neighbor Walter Stillman, also a board member, was experienced in construction.[312]

The new building was attached to the west side of the Browning School which had been built in 1908. It was designed by the firm of Sibley, Licht and Hacker, well-known school architects, and it opened in 1922. The Redfield family also established two awards to be given annually to members of the graduating class, one for mechanical drawing and the other for greatest improvement despite a handicap. Later, when the school no longer taught mechanical drawing, both were given for the latter achievement.

Architect's drawing of Tenafly High School, *The Tenakin 1927. Author's collection.*

In 1924, Malcolm S. Mackay and his sister Jennie presented thirty-one acres of land to the Tenafly Board of Education. Named Roosevelt Common in honor of Theodore Roosevelt, the property was designed to include a track and athletic field; a pond for fishing in summer and skating in winter; an outdoor theater; and space suitable for classes in forestry, agriculture and gardening as well as a simple resting space for the public. A major feature of the whole was to be a monument dedicated to the memory of Roosevelt.[313]

While a landscape architect had developed the plans, Henry Redfield was designated by the school board to monitor the progress of the Commons construction. He generally wore a distinctive crushable white felt hat. One time he remarked to Walter Stillman that he was impressed by how hard the men were working on the project whenever he came by, to which Stillman replied, "Well, Henry, it's no wonder. They can see that white hat from miles away!"[314] Construction of Roosevelt Common was completed and the monument dedicated on July 15, 1928.[315]

Henry also served as the secretary and treasurer for Grace Chapel and wrote to the missionaries the group supported in addition to sending contributions to their stipends.[316] He would ask them to bring back items from the countries they were visiting. For example, he requested Japanese prints from a missionary who was serving there. He was particularly interested in learning about architecture in other countries as well.[317]

Roosevelt Memorial, Roosevelt Common. *Author's collection.*

The Pond, Roosevelt Common. *Author's collection.*

When Alice had received her inheritance from her father in 1914, she immediately took over the management of the investments. She became an astute investor, working with a broker friend of her father's named Marshall Pasque. "She understood the market. She understood the marketplace."[318] Her brother-in-law, Harvey Wadham, a Wall Street man himself, described her as never missing anything and knowing what was going on.[319] The Stillmans were convinced that she "would have been a bank president or a corporation head had she been a man."[320]

By the early 1920s, it had become clear to all that Alice's four children appeared to be healthy and growing to a normal height, a fact that must have proved difficult for her two sisters to accept. Mary had already lost two of her own four children, and her remaining son, a hemophiliac, faced an uncertain future at best. Corinne had always considered her own short stature a severe affliction and vowed never to pass it on. Seeing that Alice's children were all of normal height for their ages apparently made her feel that her sacrifice in not attempting to have a family had been for nothing. She became bitter and gradually withdrew from contact with Alice and her family.

Dumont Clarke saw relatively little of the other Clarke family members, although he kept in contact by letters. He divided his ministry work between Manchester, Vermont, in the summers and North Carolina in the winters, working with his brother-in-law Jim McClure there. He and his wife had three children: Dumont, Phoebe Ann and James.

Lewis Clarke and his family, due to their different interests and lifestyle, had relatively little contact, and little in common with their relatives back in New Jersey. They lived in an apartment on Fifth Avenue in New York near the Metropolitan Museum. They also owned a place in Deal on the New Jersey coast.[321] When he did meet with other family members, he was usually encouraging them to join him in a speculative investment deal.[322]

He and his family enjoyed his position as president of the bank and were preoccupied with participating in the activities of the society elite. His wife, Florence, did not like visiting the Redfield home in Tenafly. She claimed the curving driveway leading up the hill to the house "scared" her. On a rare visit to their New York apartment, Stanley was given a tour of the place. He noticed some of the beds and remarked, "I shouldn't think those beds would be very comfortable." "Uncle Stanley," his niece Florence replied, "nothing here is for comfort, everything is for style."[323]

At one point, Stanley's teenage son Dumont was invited to a family luncheon at the Fifth Avenue apartment. The meal opened with a white-gloved butler presenting an ice sculpture of an elephant on a tray. The scooped-out back of the elephant was filled with caviar. After this introductory course, the only other guest, some sort of a hanger-on, asked what was coming next. When he learned it was a roast, he declared, "I don't like it!" and proceeded to go out to the kitchen and fry himself two eggs. The meal proceeded without further disruption.[324] Not surprisingly, the scene made a strong impression on the boy.

Family life in the Redfield household in Tenafly was certainly very different.

Chapter 17

REDFIELD FAMILY LIFE IN THE 1920s

When compared with that of their New York cousins, the family lifestyle of the Redfield children was much less pretentious. Alice had taken care of her housework herself for the first few years of her marriage, and cooking was one of her favorite tasks. After John's birth, she had Kate O'Hanlon to help her with the children. By the time that the family moved into the remodeled house, she had the assistance of a cook and a maid as well.[325]

Typically, the household help were Irish girls, often new immigrants, and Alice trained them as to their required duties. She was a well-liked employer, and when the girls subsequently married or decided to move on to another position, they would frequently recommend a recently arrived sister or other relative to take over their positions, so she had no difficulty in finding new help. Unlike many other employers, she allowed the girls to hold parties in the house while the family was at home if they made arrangements ahead of time, and she and Henry even came down and greeted their guests.[326]

Initially, there were two gardeners, since prior to the invention of power mowers, it took two people to mow the lawn on the four-acre property. Later, there was a single gardener who also served as a chauffeur.[327] For a number of years, the family kept chickens, and during the war, they had a cow as well, all of which the men looked after.[328]

Given the presence of both indoor and outdoor help, the children did not have any specifically assigned household tasks. They were, however expected to make their own beds and keep their rooms tidy, basically not make extra

Chickens in the yard. *Nancy Carkhuff.*

work for the household help. If they didn't always do what they should along that line, Kate O'Hanlon would usually cover for them. Louise, in particular, often needed assistance in that regard.

The family normally ate all their meals together. Every morning, Henry would read a brief Bible passage before breakfast, just a few verses long. Over the years, they went through most of the Bible that way.[329] When the children were small, if their parents were having a special event with guests, they might eat in the upstairs playroom instead.

After breakfast in the morning, Alice would go to the kitchen and discuss the day's menu with the cook and the maid. Then she would have the chauffeur drive her downtown for her daily shopping for perishable items such as meat and dairy products. Before the invention of refrigerators, they used an icebox to help preserve foods, but it was less efficient and did not keep things fresh as long.[330]

They also grew fruits and vegetables of their own on the property. Not only did they enjoy these fresh in season, but they also canned them for use during the winter. The children would help prepare for the canning by cutting up the vegetables so they were ready for cooking, which was done on the stove in the laundry.[331]

From 9:00 a.m. to noon was Alice's time to work on her financial dealings, and Kate O'Hanlon looked after the children then. She would also get them up in the morning and put them to bed at night and mind them at other times during the day as needed. She often spent time reading to them, which they particularly enjoyed.[332]

Kate O'Hanlon reading to Clarke, Louise, Ellery and John. *Alice Irizarry.*

Kate was basically treated like one of the family, rather than a servant, and stayed with them for about twenty years, until Louise and Ellery were in their teens. Generally, she got along well with Henry and Alice as well as the children, although as in any family group there were minor annoyances. Whenever someone told a story about an event, she tended to come up with another to top it. She also had difficulty with basic arithmetic, particularly involving money. Alice would get exasperated at times, as Kate apparently could not grasp the concept that if Alice owed her money, and she owed her some back, the debt could be resolved by Alice simply paying her the difference. She insisted on receiving the full amount and then paying what she owed.[333]

Alice's office was the room that had originally been intended as Henry's drafting room. However, it had proved too small for that purpose, so he had moved his drafting area up to the third floor. She had her office furnished with a telephone and a large rolltop desk at which she did all her work and in which she kept all her records.[334] The room also had a table and a couple of chairs, and she would have tea there in the afternoons, sometimes with the children.[335]

Sundays were perhaps the most highly structured days of the week. Alice had received a special recipe for cornbread from a friend. The two maids would mix up a bowl of it and place it on top of the oven before they left for early Mass at the Catholic Church. Henry would come down and place the cornbread in the oven. The family would gather around the table and he would pull out the family Bible and read from it for half an hour while the cornbread cooked. He then went out to the kitchen and brought it back, along with maple syrup, bacon and hominy to complete the meal.

After breakfast, the family went down to the chapel for the eleven o'clock Lord's Supper service. A table in the center of the room held the bread and the grape juice, as the congregation did not believe in drinking wine. Hard wooden chairs were arranged around the table, and the various families sat in their accustomed places. Alice, due to her size, had a special stool for her feet.

As noted earlier, the congregation had no minister, and the men spoke as they felt moved. The women did not speak. Mr. Kessler, who sat in front of the Redfields, started the hymns that were requested, which were sung without accompaniment. Occasionally, he might start too high for the rest of the congregation, and then his wife would try again at a lower pitch. On the rare occasions when that didn't work, it was Alice's turn to make a third try. This morning session varied from an hour to an hour and a half in length depending on how many men felt moved to speak. Henry did not speak at the meetings, but he often suggested a hymn.

The speaker for the afternoon service and his wife typically attended the morning one and frequently came home for dinner with the Redfields. The first thing Alice did when she arrived at the house was go into the kitchen to make the gravy. Although the girls had prepared the rest of the meal, she felt no one could do the gravy as well as she could. After that, dinner was ready to be served. Usually, the main course was duck, roast beef or lamb, occasionally turkey. Dessert was frequently "Floating Island," a sort of custard with meringue, or blancmange, and occasionally homemade ice cream.

After dinner, the speaker was allowed to go into the living room by himself, and the doors were closed. There he could read, rest or sleep as he chose. Meanwhile, the Redfield family went to Sunday school from 2:30 p.m. to 3:30 p.m. and then to the 4:00 p.m. afternoon service to hear the speaker. There was no evening service at that time.

Following the late-afternoon service, the speaker might occasionally come back for supper, but usually not. The children would go along for the ride while Henry drove the speaker down the Palisades to the ferry at Alpine. Their job was to shout out the car windows, "Taking a passenger! Taking a passenger!" so that other drivers waiting for the boat would not think that they were trying to jump the queue.[336]

The family's religious beliefs also affected their activities at home. Playing cards, smoking and drinking were not permitted.

Since she enjoyed rich foods and had given birth to four children, it was hardly surprising that Alice gradually grew heavier. By the late 1920s, her weight reached about 124 pounds, a significant increase over the 76 pounds she had weighed at the time of her marriage. Her figure became more or less straight up and down.

Preparing to attend her niece Katherine Wadham's wedding on a hot summer day, she hurriedly donned her own dress after getting the rest of the family members ready. Henry took one look at her and exclaimed, "Alice! That dress is so low, it's cut so deeply in the front! You cannot go over there like that!" She quickly grabbed a piece of lace and pinned it in like a dickey. Partway through the afternoon's events, she came over to her daughter and said, "Louise, can you tell what's happened? I have my dress on backwards!"[337]

Henry had created a variety of playground equipment for the children on the property. Besides a sandbox and a swing, there was a joggle board, a wide heavy board about ten feet long set between pairs of wooden posts at each end to which were attached two iron pipes close together. The board fitted between the pipes, and when the children jumped on it, it flexed, rather like a trampoline. He also made an archery target in the form of a deer out of burlap stuffed with straw with four stick legs and antlers. The children regularly enjoyed shooting the deer with bows and arrows. They also had a hut in the woods that they used frequently.[338]

Reading was encouraged. In addition to a well-stocked library, the family subscribed to *St. Nicholas* magazine for the children, and magazines like *Popular Mechanics*, which were of general interest.[339]

Alice's interest in and appreciation for osteopathy, originally developed during her stay in Kirksville, continued throughout her life. Initially, she had an osteopath come out from New York City on a fairly regular basis to treat whatever was bothering a family member at the time. As long as the osteopath was at the house anyway, she would offer other family members or friends the opportunity to have a little treatment as well, and they generally felt they benefited from it. She even had a regular osteopath's table kept in the upstairs sitting room.[340] When John developed headaches, perhaps a result from his crossed eyes, he found the treatments most beneficial.[341] Later on, the family used the services of local New Jersey osteopaths.

In July 1923, Clarke and John, along with their parents, traveled by car to Buffalo, New York. From there, they embarked on an eight-day lake cruise to Duluth and back before driving back home.[342] Clarke attended various summer camps in other years.

Clarke was one of the original fifteen students who started their freshman year at the new Tenafly High School in February 1922 before the building was fully completed.[343] He and some friends began the Ham Radio Club at the school, and it soon morphed into the Science Club, for which he served as president from his sophomore through his senior years.[344] His interest in ham radio continued throughout his life.

In his junior and senior years, he served as class treasurer and took part in Kinsprits. During his senior year, he was also an assistant on the *The Tenakin* staff,[345] a member of the Varsity Club, a participant in track and manager for the basketball team. He graduated in February 1926, earned a degree in engineering in 1929 and went to work for Western Electric.

John entered the new Tenafly High School in 1923. He served as a member of the school orchestra, playing the flute all four years he was there. He spent some time as a member of the Chess Club, Science Club and Camera Club as well. In his senior year, he served as manager for the baseball team.[346] Like Clarke, he attended summer camps a number of years.

In August 1925, shortly before his sixteenth birthday, he had an operation to correct his cross-eyed condition.[347] Interestingly, the man who performed it, Dr. Frank X. Brophy, was the son of John Brophy, who had served as coachman for the Clarke family years before.[348] Unfortunately, due to John's age at the time of the operation, he was never able to see using both eyes at once, so he still had no depth perception. After graduating from high school in 1927, John enrolled in New York University to study business and finance.

Dumont Clarke III, Stanley's son, graduated from Tenafly High School that same year, although his first two years of high school were spent elsewhere. At Tenafly High, he belonged to the Drama Club and played football, serving as manager of the team his senior year. He was also the school's movie operator and president of the senior class.[349]

Meanwhile, in 1919, shortly before her fourth birthday, Louise had started spending mornings at a school run by Miss Lucille Cornish in Englewood. She soon learned how to form letters and do simple addition.[350] Unfortunately, in May 1920, she developed an infected gland in her neck. A doctor operated and inserted a drain in the wound, but it was slow to heal, and the drain remained in place for seven months until it finally closed over.[351] Alice kept her at home for a while and taught her herself.[352] Later, she was unable to send her back to school, as she herself could not drive and, at that time, lacked a chauffeur. She hired Miss Helen Wendover to teach Louise at home.

Miss Wendover was an excellent young teacher who had unfortunately lost one of her hands in a train accident while she was a child. As a result, she had a wooden prosthetic hand she kept covered with a glove. Being a curious child, young Louise asked her why she always wore the glove and then was most sorry and embarrassed when she learned the reason.[353] Louise did well with her, and by the time she was six and a half, she had learned her multiplication tables.[354] She subsequently started attending the Tenafly Public School, beginning in Grade 2B in the fall of 1922.[355]

Early on, when the older children were playing outside, Louise could often be found sitting quietly on the joggle board going jiggle, jiggle, jiggle.[356] Indoors in the playroom, if Louise asked the boys to play dolls with her, they generally ended up doing something like declaring the dolls to be "sick" and sticking pins into them to treat them.[357] She soon gave up on the dolls and became a bit of a tomboy. Since the stage in the playroom was raised, they would sometimes place a board against it so they could run toy cars down the slope. They also frequently used the stage to put on plays, charging the audience members a cherry or a penny to watch them.[358]

At one point, Louise asked her mother why one of the neighbor girls had so many nice things that she didn't, fancier clothes, ballet lessons and the like. Alice replied that not only was that girl an only child but also the things that her own family had were paid for, while the other girl's things were not.[359] When she tried wheedling on her father, his response was that her mother had "the best common sense in the whole wide world" and she should just listen to her.[360]

It seems likely that Ellery began his education at the Tenafly Public School, probably at about the same time that Louise started there, as he would have been five years old by then. Being ten years younger than Clarke and eight years younger than John, he had little in common with them. He is described as being something of a rebel, independent and determined. At the same time, he appeared to have a warm, friendly outgoing personality. He frequently got into scrapes. At one point, after climbing up a cherry tree, he fell out and broke his arm.[361]

Since she was older, Katherine Stillman was sometimes delegated to keep an eye on him. On one occasion when Alice and Henry were getting ready to take the family to an important function, Louise and Ellery were dressed and ready first, so to keep them out of mischief while the others got ready, they were sent on a car ride with Katherine and the family chauffeur. The chauffeur decided to treat them all to chocolate ice cream cones. Whether accidentally or on purpose, Ellery promptly succeeded in smearing his all the way down his front.[362] On another occasion, when the family decided to visit the Statue of Liberty, he insisted on walking up the stairs rather than taking the elevator like everyone else, so Katherine had to walk up with him.[363]

The children enjoyed sports, particularly swimming and tennis, and both were available at the Crowe's Nest in Summit, New York, where the family usually spent a few weeks most summers. Guests there were welcomed on arrival and saluted on departure by the ringing of a big dinner bell. The Crowe's Nest had its own private beach with a small dock. One time, Louise stayed too long in the water and got chilled, then proceeded to gorge herself on potato salad at dinner and became very ill as a result. She spent the rest of the night sleeping on the box spring of her bed after she and her mother threw the mattress out the window to get rid of the mess.[364]

The Crowes Nest, Summit, New York. *Author's collection.*

Uncle Stanley was a favorite with the children, and they looked forward to seeing him when he came to visit, which he did fairly frequently, though usually by himself, as he and Alice were quite close. He often arrived with a supply of fresh Tootsie Rolls, and although Henry didn't really approve, he would bring along copies of the newspaper comics and read them to the children, putting in all the *Zams! Booms!* and *Pops!* and explaining any details that they did not understand.[365]

Carving peach pits, one of Stanley's hobbies, they also found intriguing. Usually he created a variety of imaginary faces, but sometimes he chose to depict animals as well.[366]

As time went on, Alice and her family tended to see less of her other Clarke relatives. Lewis's family continued to focus on their high-society life. Although the Cases lived in nearby Englewood, visiting tended to be a bit awkward and did not occur often, as the children had to be careful around the Cases' son Robert due to his hemophilia.

Since Alice's brother Dumont II and his family divided their time between their home in Manchester, Vermont, and Annie's brother James's place in North Carolina, there was less opportunity for them to visit, although Alice and Dumont corresponded regularly. Corrine gradually became more estranged.

Thus Alice and her family tended to see more of their Redfield relatives than of their Clarke ones. Of course, Henry's sister Katherine Wadham and her family lived just down the street. Henry's mother and his two unmarried sisters, Louise and Daisy, lived together in Tenafly, and they saw each other regularly. His older brother, Herbert, and his large family lived in Closter nearby. Henry and Alice hosted Redfield family reunions for them all on a couple of occasions.

Chapter 18

FLOATING UNIVERSITY

John Redfield completed his first year of study at New York University in the spring of 1928 and then decided to take part in a special program. A psychology professor at the university, James Edwin Lough, had come up with the concept of a Floating University, a vessel on which a group of students and teachers would travel around the world together, stopping off for a time in various countries along the route, getting to meet the people there and see the sights. While onboard ship, they would take a series of courses that would help them to better understand the people and places they were going to visit and receive college credit for their efforts.

When initially planned, the project was to be under the auspices of New York University, but it failed to attract sufficient participants to be viable. Subsequently, Lough formed the University Travel Association with the assistance of a Greek student, Constantine Raises, and opened the program to students of all colleges and universities. Applications came in from students at 143 colleges in 40 states plus some from Canada, Cuba and Hawaii. The association chartered one of the Holland America Line's older passenger vessels, the SS *Ryndam*, to carry the university from place to place and serve as a base. The first group, comprising 504 students and a faculty and administrative staff of 63, set sail on September 18, 1926. Over a period of seven and a half months, they traveled 41,000 miles and visited 35 countries and more than 90 cities.[367] A photo caption promoting the second voyage for the program indicated that the *Ryndam* would set sail on September 20, 1927, with a faculty of 35 and a student body of 375.[368]

Students riding an elephant, from the First Floating University. Promotional photo for the Second Floating University. *Author's collection.*

John joined the Floating University for its third year, 1928–29. The group left New York on the first leg of its voyage on November 8, 1928, aboard the Dollar Line's SS *President Wilson*. Approximately one hundred students from all over the country took part in the expedition. Most, like John, were in the early stages of their college careers. Presumably due to the smaller size of the group, chartering the *Ryndam* for the entire voyage was no longer a viable option.

The group comprised 110 individuals in all. Constantine Raises served as cruise director. The faculty consisted of eleven officers of instruction, a number of whom were professors at prestigious institutions, including Stanford, Princeton and Mount Holyoke, among others. Many served dual roles as administrators as well. Sidney Greenbie, the president of the group, led the expedition. His wife, Marjorie Greenbie, served as assistant director of education in charge of women. Subjects available from which students could select a course of study included sociology, literature, geology, geography, philosophy, education, journalism, religions, art, literature, history, government, economics and foreign languages: French, German, Spanish and Greek.[369]

From New York, the group was to proceed to Cuba, through Panama, to California and Hawaii, then on to Japan, China and the Philippines, Penang and Singapore. Java, Siam and Burma came next. Then it was on to India, Egypt, Palestine, Syria, Cyprus and Turkey. Finally, they were to spend two months in continental Europe, visiting Greece, Italy, Austria, Czechoslovakia, Germany, France and Switzerland, arriving back in New York on June 11, 1929.[370]

Unfortunately, no direct personal record of John's experiences on the trip survives. However, he appears fairly extensively in the letters written home from the voyage by Lucy Bancroft, a young lady from Walnut Creek, California, who had just completed her first year at Stanford University. It is unclear how they became acquainted, but it's possible they met through Lucy's roommate on the first leg of the voyage. She was a friend of Kit Vinson, a young man from Houston, Texas, who was a roommate of John's. Lucy and Kit frequently played deck tennis together on the *President Wilson*.[371]

When John first arrived in Japan, he received a concerned cable from his parents, who had not heard from him in a number of weeks. They had failed to take into account that due to being at sea, letters he wrote on board would not be mailed until the ship reached port. Since cables cost a dollar a word and one had to pay for the address as well, practical John wrote back the briefest response he could come up with: "All well love Redfield Tenafly."[372]

John first appears in Lucy's letters in one describing Christmas Eve in Kyoto, Japan. She, John and a group of friends were out taking an evening walk. Another boy had been teased by some other students earlier, falsely telling him he could not go on the Java trip, which had a limited number of spots available. Not part of the group of friends, he suddenly ran up from behind them and angrily accosted John before running off. A short time later, he came running out of an alley and attacked John with a clasp knife. John warded him off and turned his back to talk to some of the others. The assailant then tried to stab John in the back, but Lucy grabbed his hand, so he turned on her instead. Fortunately, the others promptly came to her aid, hitting the attacker hard enough to stun him. He burst into tears and ran off.[373] When they reported the incident to the faculty, they learned the faculty had known beforehand that the young man was a "mental case."[374] Surprisingly, he was not sent home as a result, although some other students had been dismissed for unruly drunken behavior.

Lucy joined the small group of about twenty students who were going to Java, while John went with the main group to China. When the two groups met up again in Singapore, there was considerable upset. The

John Redfield aboard the
USS *President Wilson* for the
Third Floating University.
Author's collection.

group returning from Java had had to share their vessel with a large cargo of pigs. The smell was so bad and the staterooms so dirty that they were forced to sleep on deck.[375] A number of the young women on the China trip had been behaving questionably, picking up "port men" at various stops, drinking and staying out late, which disgusted other members of the group. Mrs. Greenbie apparently didn't want to be labeled "out of date" and allowed most anything. Dr. Greenbie was away making arrangements for later portions of the trip. The faculty was in an uproar, and some refused to attend meetings. The dean of men resigned. One of the remaining professors took over and restored order.[376] None of the drama seemed to bother Lucy and her friends unduly. They remained focused on getting the most out of the trip.

As time went on, Lucy, Kit and John, along with a few others, began more and more frequently to do things together as a group. Those two were her special friends. "Kit and John are so much fun to quarrel with, to tease, and have a good time with. John is a couple of months younger than I, but is really much younger, he'd have a fit if he knew I thought so, but that doesn't matter."[377] John's fundamentalist religious background compared to her less restrictive one was probably a factor in her observation. She later notes, "It is real grand to have John and Kit as friends, for I can be with either or both as much as we please, and no one talks too much."[378]

While in Bangkok, John Decker, the history professor, the youngest faculty member and one of their group of friends, invited them to go with him to take tea with the chief justice of the Siamese Court. He had gone to school with the man's son-in-law.[379] At other stops along the trip, they met various ambassadors and government ministers as part of a series of formal welcomes for the Floating University. Their activities were sometimes covered in the local press as well.

Although some people on the expedition appeared to want to have everything simply handed to them, by the time they reached India, Lucy and her friends realized that much of what they would get out of the experience would depend on the effort they put into it themselves. On a day in Calcutta when there were no official Floating University events scheduled, she and her friends arranged their own program, visiting a memorial, the Indian Museum, a palace and a Jain temple and lab where students were working on studying the feelings of inanimate objects.[380]

India offered many contrasting sights and experiences. From a boat trip on the Ganges, they were disturbed to watch "lepers, deformed people, rich and poor all slopping that filthy water over their thin bodies in an extacy [*sic*] of religious zeal." A snake-charming group put on an act where a mongoose attacked a snake and appeared to kill it and the snake charmer brought it back to life. In Delhi, they took a guided tour led by some Sikh students from Delhi University who later invited Lucy, John and Kit back to their quarters for a dinner in their traditional style. There they also got to see Mahatma Gandhi, who was passing through by train and made a brief stop to greet an assembled crowd. Lucy shook hands with him. In Agra, Kit and John woke Lucy before dawn to join them in going to view the Taj Mahal by moonlight. Over the next eighteen hours, they viewed it by sunrise, midday, sunset and starlight. She declared it the most beautiful sight she had ever seen.[381]

On the long train trip from Bombay to Madras, Lucy was surprised to discover that Kit and John and a couple of other boys did not know how to play poker, so she and another friend decided to teach them. While they were at it, they taught them how to play hearts and blackjack plus a couple of other card games. When in Madras, Lucy received a letter from her mother, in which, among other things, she asked what Lucy had been doing at the time her mother was writing to her. John, who liked to work with figures, calculated that their group had been crossing the equator then.[382]

Back onboard ship on the way to Cairo, classes resumed. In addition to their own studies, Lucy, Kit and John audited some of one another's classes. In their spare time, Lucy and John played chess, at which he was clearly superior, and checkers, where Lucy generally prevailed. They tried to teach Kit chess, but he was not particularly enthusiastic about it. Student council meetings revolved around dissatisfaction with various aspects of the trip. A number of promised stops had been missed. At times, accommodations were of substandard quality. Times to be spent at the various sites on the upcoming European portion of the tour were too short. Many people were getting crabby and starting to call one another names. Lucy and her friends decided to ignore them as far as possible.[383]

In Cairo, they started by taking a short trip out of the city to get a brief look at the scenery. Then they drove by car the next day to Memphis. From there, they rode camels out to see the pyramids and sphinx up close in detail. Lucy, who was accustomed to riding horses on her father's farm back home, was impressed by how different and bone shaking riding a camel could be. She gave a detailed comparison of its gaits with those of a horse. Noting that she had some difficulty trying to adjust to the change, she concluded, "Camels seem to lack all sense of coordination."

Camel riding proved even harder on John and some of the others who were not accustomed to riding at all. By the end of the seventeen-and-a-half-mile journey, their party formed a long, spread out group of stragglers. It took those in the rear like John more than an hour to catch up with the rest of the group, which had gathered at the home of an Arab leader. There they enjoyed a meal of mutton stew, using bread rather than utensils to scoop up the food. Lucy bemoaned the fact that Kit and John, stiff from the camel riding, were dubious about taking another trip the following day.[384]

Then it was on to Luxor and a donkey ride to the Valley of the Kings where they saw not only the tombs of Rameses II and III but also King Tut's tomb, which was specially opened for them. Through a pass they entered the Valley of the Queens and visited one of the tombs there, followed by a temple. Finally, they headed back to Cairo by train.[385]

Next came a brief tour of the Holy Land, followed by a cruise around the east Mediterranean, traveling on the ship at night and making various side trips at ports in Turkey, Cyprus and Syria during the days.

Then it was on to Athens. After seeing the condition of the Acropolis, Lucy felt heartily glad that Lord Elgin had rescued the marbles, although what remained, particularly the Parthenon and the Porch of the Maidens, plus the temple gateway of Zeus, she found most impressive.[386] She and her group of friends posed for a picture in a ruined theater there.

Another dramatic blowup from the dissatisfied students occurred while the group was still in Athens. Lucy spoke up against them and discovered that more members of the group shared her views than she had realized. John Decker was put in charge of things during Mr. Greenbie's absence, which pleased her, as she felt he would not put up with any nonsense.

The next stop was Naples, where the group spent a scant two days. On the first day they drove the Amalfi-Sorrento Drive, visited the aquarium and had tea with the local count and countess. Then it was on to the Grand Opera for a performance of *Tosca*. On the second day, they visited Vesuvius and Pompeii.

Pompeii fascinated Lucy, though she described it as "creepy" as well, particularly the petrified bodies of the inhabitants. The ancient wine and bread shops differed little from the modern ones she saw in Naples. Election

John Redfield, Lucy Bancroft and friends at a theater on the Acropolis, Athens, Greece. *Author's collection.*

posters and pictures on the walls of the buildings looked like new. She and three of her friends got separated from the rest of the group, trying to poke around and see as much as possible. Fortunately, they were reunited on the train back to Naples before the conductor discovered they had neither money nor their passes, which were held by the leaders of the main group.[387]

Vienna proved to be a combination of the old and the new. Lucy did not particularly care for the new art deco–style art and architecture. She much preferred the old wine cellars, castles and palaces in the area. She noted that the conflict between the old order and modern socialism there was creating some unrest.

Most of John's friends on the trip were smokers, so it was hardly surprising that he finally decided to try smoking himself. Since he found he enjoyed the experience, he asked Lucy to join him on a shopping trip in search of a lighter.[388]

John Decker arranged an informal tea for his history students with the Austrian Minister of Foreign Affairs on May 7. Although Lucy was only auditing the course, she was able to go along with Kit, John and Mickey, who were taking it for credit.[389] They thoroughly enjoyed the tea and found their conversation with the minister most interesting, staying until he finally had to leave for another engagement.

After dinner, she and her group of friends went off to an amusement park to celebrate her birthday. Knowing that loop-the-loop rides tended to make her ill, she avoided them for most of the evening. However, John finally persuaded her and the others to try one, with unfortunately predictable results. John was unaffected. She had to be assisted back to the hotel, where she flopped miserably on her bed while John packed her bags for their early departure the next day. He then left to join the others for ice cream and chocolate, while she groaned at the very thought.[390]

Apparently, about the time that the group reached Berlin on May 15, the dissatisfaction of the disgruntled student faction came to a head. John Decker had found it necessary to dismiss two of the faculty, and those two, along with about fifteen of the students, determined to "financially and socially wreck the Greenbies." They released several uncomplimentary articles to the American press and boasted that their grievances were going to be featured in a Sunday supplement. Lucy was very upset.[391] John Decker initially put a stop to things, but when Mr. Greenbie rejoined the group, the situation boiled over.[392]

A newspaper clipping from the front page of the *San Francisco Examiner* with a dateline of Paris, May 21, went over some of the students' allegations in detail.[393] They complained of substandard accommodations in hotels with questionable reputations, claiming they were dives and opium dens, when they had been promised first class, not to mention the filth and discomfort in India, and the odorous return trip to Singapore the Java group was forced to make on a ship loaded with 2,200 hogs. They claimed the supposed education component of the voyage completely broke down. Students who fell ill were left to their own devices to attempt to rejoin the group, and some had to resort to seeking help from local American consuls. When asked if they felt they lacked freedom, they complained that rather they were left to their own devices too much.

Lucy reassured her family:

> All the publicity you see is greatly overdone, whether it says that we had to lie down with our camels in a sandstorm while riding the 30 yards from the trolley station to the base of the furtherest [sic] pyramid, or whether it states that all the girls are immoral gold diggers, and all of the boys Don Juans. My letters have been as frank and honest as I could make them, and as full.[394]

From Paris, the group proceeded to Switzerland. John Decker and Mildred Harrington, his girlfriend, had become engaged and decided to remain there to marry, as the country required only a twenty-day waiting period for them to do so. The remaining members of the Floating University proceeded on to Marseilles, where they boarded the *President Wilson* for the trip home.

Lucy's final letter written on board ship waxed nostalgic about the experience: "The companionship I've had from Mickey, Kit, John and the others, I wouldn't trade for all of my illusions." At the same time, she wondered whether, given all the unfavorable publicity, a fourth Floating University would actually take place.[395]

Sidney Greenbie, in an optimistic promotional letter for the fourth voyage written in early 1929, after praising the current participants, expressed his confidence based on his experiences: "Knowing now just the kind of students that make the happiest grouping, and having but two hundred to register, knowing now the best kind of faculty to pick for Floating University, we look forward to a better, more fruitful year for 1929–30."[396]

Despite the difficulties experienced on the third voyage, a fourth voyage did apparently take place, although whether it actually lived up to those glowing prognostications seems unlikely. A fifth voyage was also proposed

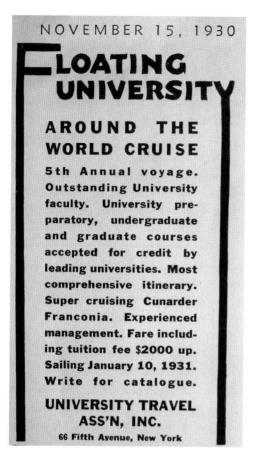

NOVEMBER 15, 1930

FLOATING UNIVERSITY

AROUND THE WORLD CRUISE

5th Annual voyage. Outstanding University faculty. University preparatory, undergraduate and graduate courses accepted for credit by leading universities. Most comprehensive itinerary. Super cruising Cunarder Franconia. Experienced management. Fare including tuition fee $2000 up. Sailing January 10, 1931. Write for catalogue.

UNIVERSITY TRAVEL ASS'N, INC.

66 Fifth Avenue, New York

Advertisement for the Fifth Floating University. Unidentified publication. *Author's collection.*

in an advertisement published on November 15, 1930.[397] If it did, in fact, take place, it was likely the last. With the stock market crash in the fall of 1929 and the deepening Depression of the early 1930s, fewer people were in a position to consider participating, and the unfortunate reputation of the earlier voyage certainly did not help.

Nevertheless, many of the members of the third voyage retained positive memories of their experiences, and a twenty-fifth reunion of the group in 1954 was well attended. After John returned from the trip, out of respect for his father, he neither smoked nor played cards at home, although he indulged in both activities elsewhere.

Chapter 19

CHANGING TIMES, CHANGING LIVES

While John was away, his father was busy working on the construction of a new home for the growing congregation of Grace Chapel. Washington Hall on Washington Street was no longer adequate to meet their needs. They decided to move that building a block and a half away and construct a new enlarged meeting area attached to it. Henry Redfield, as he had done for other local public construction projects, acted as overseer.

But Henry was not well. His niece Katherine Wadham recalled visiting the chapel one day while he was inspecting the new baptistery designed for full immersions. After he climbed out, he was feeling faint and lay down across a group of chairs. She realized he must be ill. Soon after, Henry went to the doctor, who performed an exploratory operation and discovered he had inoperable cancer of the liver. There was nothing to be done.[398] Alice obtained a hospital bed and hired a nurse to help look after him at home. If he felt up to it, he would go out and sit in the garden on the north side of the house. When the Stillman children asked if they could visit him, their mother told them that it was all right to go and talk with him, but not to stay too long because he would get too tired.[399]

Shortly before he died, Henry advised his daughter, "Now Louise, I don't want you to wear black, because it looks too smashing on blondes. If you'd like to wear white for a while, that'll be fine. But white is very hard to keep clean, so be sure you do all the wash yourself and don't make too much work for your mother."[400]

Clarke and Alice on the front lawn steps. *Author's collection.*

On July 3, 1931 at age fifty-seven, Henry passed away. Unfortunately, at his funeral, his mother fell and broke her hip. Despite her own grief, Alice remained gracious and practical. "The nurse is here, we'll just keep her," she decided, and she did for the next few months until Lavinia could get around by herself again.[401] Having her mother-in-law's needs to focus on helped

Alice through that difficult time. However, even after a normal period of mourning, Alice continued to wear black clothing almost exclusively for the rest of her life.

Meanwhile, her sister Corinne refused to attend Henry's funeral. She claimed she couldn't be a hypocrite.[402] She apparently had come to resent Alice's happy marriage and productive lifestyle. Her behavior was becoming stranger and contrasted starkly with the attitudes of others.

Alice received many letters of condolence. Among them was one from Malcolm S. MacKay, the donor of the property for Roosevelt Common:

> *I know very well that what anyone may write in times like you are going through helps very little. However, I can not [sic] refrain from telling you in what high regard I held your late husband. He seemed to be one of those rare men who had a vision of how things could be rendered more beautiful and of greater service to all men. And his clear mind and all seeing spirit ever pushed him on in its accomplishment—Particularly did I appreciate his service to Roosevelt Common—No man did more to make that Playground what it is than he did—And I and all those associated with him will always honor him for it.*
>
> *Life after all is not to be measured in years, but in accomplishment, And in the faith and vision that your spirit has held up to others.*
>
> *May God be very close to you, and give you strength and peace.[403]*

In 1933, Alice donated trees to Roosevelt Common in memory of Henry, and the board of education named the natural theater there the Henry W. Redfield Outdoor Theatre.[404]

The loss of his father was a great tragedy for Clarke. He had prayed and prayed that his father would not die, to no avail. He was quite depressed and withdrawn for some time.[405] He attempted to play the role of a father to his younger siblings, but Louise would have none of it. Ellery, only fourteen at the time, was away at summer camp when his father died and did not learn of his passing until he returned home. Needless to say, he was very upset as a result. John and Louise felt the loss of their father keenly as well.

Fortunately, due to Alice's skillful and prudent management, her family did not suffer any significant financial stress as a result of the Great Depression and the loss of her husband. All four of her children continued to live at home with her.

The family also had two dogs at the time. Ellery had rescued one, a small terrier mix, after it got its tail caught and broken in the front door

Pickles on the front porch. *John Redfield.*

of the bank downtown. They christened it Pickles, and it soon became Alice's personal pet.[406] At the same time, Clarke had a Russian wolfhound, a beautiful dog, but not very smart. The two of them would chase rabbits together. The wolfhound could make great leaps but not turn corners, so it was up to Pickles to herd the rabbit into the corner of the fence so they could catch it. Once they had it, they didn't quite know what to do with it, and it usually ended up getting away. But watching the chase provided amusing entertainment.[407]

Pickles became quite a character around town. He would go from door to door, begging. One family might give him a piece of bacon, another, a slice of toast. Finally, he would end up at Henry's mother's place and rest a while. When Alice thought it time for him to come home, she would call and say, "Bring Pickles to the phone." When he got there, she would tell him, "Pickles, come home!" and he would run to the door and head for home as fast as he could go.[408]

New York University did not grant John credit for his time on the Floating University, so he had to earn alternate credits when he returned. He commuted into New York City to attend his college classes with a group of half a dozen friends. They paid six cents each to ride the trolley from Tenafly to Wall Street in lower Manhattan. To get from there farther uptown to the university required an additional four-cent fee. They would give their pennies to one member of the group to drop into the fare box all at once and charge on through, to the great annoyance of the coin collector.[409]

While John continued his studies, he joined Theta Chi Fraternity. The young men soon realized that their fraternity house could benefit from a woman's touch, so they decided to form a Mothers Club to achieve this, without putting a strain on their chapter treasury. Alice went with John to the first meeting of the group. He wondered what their reaction would be to her size, and while there was initially some surprise, within a few minutes, no one continued to think anything about it. She worked with the Mothers Club for a number of years.[410]

Having thoroughly enjoyed the Floating University experience, John kept in contact with the friends he had made there, Lucy Bancroft in particular. She completed her studies at Stanford and then proceeded to take some graduate courses in education at Berkley. Subsequently, she came east to continue her graduate education at Columbia University in New York.[411] She later served as a governess for a young boy.

John graduated from New York University in 1932 and spent the next two years looking for a job in banking in New York City. He would go into town once a week and make the rounds of the Wall Street banks to see whether they had any positions open. He was hoping for a position in international banking, but none was available.[412] People who actually already had a job during the Depression generally were much more interested in holding onto it than risking changing positions.

In 1933, Louise Redfield graduated from Tenafly High School, where she had been very active in extracurricular activities. In addition to participating in the Glee Club and the County Chorus, she had worked on the Spring Festival and took part in theater productions every year. Her junior and senior years she worked on Mardi Gras. She played basketball for three years then switched to soccer as a senior. In addition to all that, she served as senior class secretary, a member of the Awards Committee, and was selected a member of the National Honor Society.[413] She went on to attend Goucher College in Towson, Maryland. Her uncle Dumont's daughter, Phoebe Ann, was a student there, so Alice thought it a suitable school for Louise.[414]

In the spring of 1934, John's persistent job search finally paid off. On one of his weekly rounds, he stopped to leave an application at Bankers

John Redfield with his fraternity brothers. *Author's collection.*

Trust Company. A day or two later, an employee in foreign collections quit unexpectedly. The man searching for a replacement knew of John and contacted him directly. Thanks to his travels with the Floating University, he knew something about foreign currencies and a bit about foreign exchange, and as a result, he was hired.[415] He ended up working for the bank in various different capacities for the next thirty years.

Ellery graduated from Tenafly High in 1935, but little is known of his time there, other than that he played the bassoon in the school band.[416] Rather than listing his achievements, his high school yearbook merely gives a quote from him, "Hold the fort, I'm coming."[417] He continued to get into various scrapes, one of which was particularly stressful for Alice.

Ellery was dating a girl, Eileen Eversley, with a troubled background. Her parents were divorced, and she was not living with either of them but staying in a house down at the end of Engle Street. Behind the house was a steep gully with a brook at the bottom that had been dammed to form a large pond. One evening, Ellery and Eileen were necking in the car behind the house above the pond. Somehow, the brake became disengaged, and the car ended up in the water. Alice received a call from the police that Ellery was having a problem. He returned home both wet and chagrined, and the car had to be towed out.

Alice was very upset by the incident. She paced back and forth up and down the living room saying, "I just can't take it alone. I can't do it alone." And all of a sudden, it was just like someone reached right down to touch her on her shoulder and said, "You're not alone. You've never been alone." And from then on, she never felt out of control again.[418]

While Alice's financial skills proved important for the welfare of her own family, for her, they were not an end in themselves. Rather, she "enjoyed moneymaking, just for what it could do, more than for the ability to accumulate, which is a very, very, different talent."[419] She became seriously involved in helping her friends and neighbors during the hard times brought on by the Depression.

Her friend Julia Russell, whom she had visited while abroad in England back in 1903, had subsequently been widowed and returned to New Jersey. When she ran low on funds, she decided to sell some of her Irish husband's family heirlooms she had brought back with her. Alice bought them from her at their full market value, a practice she adhered to in all her dealings with those she aided.[420]

A lady living down on Magnolia Street, Mrs. Ballard, had lost her husband to tuberculosis. Her son had passed away earlier. She was all alone and needed funds. Alice bought her house so she would have money to look after herself. She then turned it into two apartments, which she rented out for a number of years.[421]

Word of Alice's generosity got around. One of her neighbors who had lost his job in New York City was returning home to New Jersey. While crossing the bridge over the Hudson River, he thought seriously about committing suicide by jumping. Then he reconsidered. He believed his main problem in finding a new job was that he had lost all his teeth and appeared older and more decrepit than he actually was. If he asked Mrs. Redfield for a loan to purchase false teeth, he might be able to find employment again. He went and spoke to her. She gave him the loan, and he did indeed get a new job.[422]

Alice did not simply give out money casually to anyone who asked. There had to be an appropriate purpose for the funds requested and a reasonable plan for reimbursement if the transaction was a loan—although due to unforeseen circumstances, that might not always work out.[423]

In addition to helping out individuals, she assisted local businesses as well. Demarest's Hardware in Tenafly always stocked up on toys for the Christmas season, as did many other retailers. Knowing this, toy manufacturers tended to increase their prices in the fall. If retailers could afford to purchase the toys earlier in the year, they could get them at a better price and realize a greater profit during the holiday season. Alice loaned the business money to buy the toys out of season, and they both profited.[424]

However, not all her efforts produced quite the results she intended. One of Clarke's friends had become a dentist. He was a fine young man she knew well, and she determined to help him get a good start in business by going to him herself and urging all her friends to do so. Inadvertently, she almost bankrupted him. He had intended to work on only adults' teeth originally. However, Alice's mouth was so small that he had to go out right away and get a loan to purchase some expensive equipment designed for use on children. Fortunately, everything worked out in the end since she sent so many of her friends to him.[425]

Charitable institutions also received her support. Before her marriage, she had helped at the Rethmore Home, which provided a fresh-air experience for underprivileged children from the city. Later, she worked with the Mary Fisher Home, an organization established to look after elderly and needy professional individuals—schoolteachers, artists, actors and the like. Some who entered the home gave it all their worldly goods in exchange for support. In other cases, family members paid for the resident's care. Some who lacked funds to pay for their accommodations provided services in kind to the home. Fundraising events were also held to help defray costs.

Founded in 1888 by Mary A. Fisher in New York City, the organization was originally called the Home Hotel and housed in a Brooklyn property owned by Mary Fisher's father. Later it changed its name to the Mary Fisher Home to avoid confusion with regular hotel businesses. Mary Fisher served as the original president of the Mary Fisher Home Association and lived in the home to supervise its operation. As the number of its clients expanded, it moved to a variety of different rental locations within the New York City area. In 1899, the organization opened a second home in Tenafly on Jay Street (later named River Edge Road) at the request of subscribers and applicants living in the New Jersey area. The original Mary Fisher Home, thanks to legacies and donations, was able to construct its first permanent residence in Mount Vernon, New York, in 1911–12. With that building's completion, Mary Fisher resigned from the board and moved to the Tenafly Home.

In 1915, she published a book describing the history of the home up to that point, at least in part in hope of raising funds for a new Tenafly building.[426] In 1923, the Tenafly home moved to the former Waddell mansion on Engle Street at Forest Road.[427]

The original Mary Fisher Home in Tenafly. *Author's collection.*

It is unclear when Alice first took an interest the Mary Fisher Home. She is not mentioned in Mary Fisher's book, but she definitely was working with the home by the mid-1920s. Possibly she became involved with the organization about the time that it moved to Engle Street. As with most of the organizations she worked with, she served as treasurer due to her financial background.

When John had his eye operation in 1925, one of the ladies living at the home volunteered to visit and read to him, as he was not allowed to read by himself for a time. Unfortunately for him, she was only interested in the WCTU (Woman's Christian Temperance Union), so he ended up hearing quite a bit of information about the organization's board members and the evils of demon rum.[428]

Alice also worked with the Tenafly Civic and Welfare Organization, of which she was one of the founders. This organization was designed to provide temporary assistance to people in crisis situations. They might need coal for the winter or be temporarily short on food. Or a family might have a child that desperately needed glasses but couldn't afford them. She and a couple of others, along with the poor mistress in town, got together and set up the organization. From some people, they received money gifts, but

Alice also went around to the local butchers and grocers and coal merchants soliciting donations.[429]

Not all of the assistance Alice provided to others involved financial matters. Sometimes she just provided a confidential sympathetic listening ear. Mrs. Elizabeth Rosebaugh, the wife of the Episcopal minister, would come to talk with her periodically to vent her frustrations with some of the difficulties she had with her parishioners. She knew Alice was a good Christian who understood exactly how she felt. She could get everything off her chest and knew it would never go any further. Sometimes Alice was even able to help her find a solution for some of her problems.[430]

Alice's brother Dumont, who had been dividing his time between Manchester, Vermont, and Asheville, North Carolina, moved his family permanently to Asheville in 1930. His brother-in-law, Jim McClure, had formed a Farmers' Federation Cooperative to help the local farmers pool their resources to gain better prices for their products. The group developed warehouses and chicken hatcheries among other things to help serve their members who owned stock in the cooperative as well.

Jim McClure decided to introduce the concept of the Lord's Acre to his federation in 1927. Based on an plan developed earlier by a minister in Georgia, the idea was that each farmer should set aside the products of one acre of his land to support the church, maybe an acre of cotton, or corn or potatoes, or, if into livestock, raise a steer or a hog or provide a portion of his chickens' egg production for the purpose. Initially, the idea received only a small response that soon petered out. Someone was needed to take the project in hand and sustain it.

He persuaded Dumont Clarke to move to North Carolina and take on the work of building up the country church. "Spearheaded by Dumont's unflagging determination and missionary zeal, the Lord's Acre plan not only answered the needs of impoverished rural churches in western North Carolina, but also came into use in many parts of the United States and even spread to the mission field worldwide."[431]

Corinne continued to be outspoken and at times dictatorial. In Demarest, she served on the school board and in the Baptist Church, and for much of her life she was on the board of the Englewood Hospital as well.[432] She either liked people or detested them, with no real half measures, and they returned the favor. Sadly, sooner or later, most people ended up in the second category.

When her brother Dumont came back north to visit the other members of the family from time to time, she made it very clear to him that if he

Jim McClure and Dumont Clarke presenting the Lord's Acre Movement. Promotional photo for their work. *Author's collection.*

were to visit Alice and her family, she would not see him. Alice and Dumont continued to keep in contact through correspondence.[433]

Through her work at the Englewood Hospital, Corinne came to admire some of the young professional men there. She took to giving them presents and even taking them off on trips, but when they married, she would drop them like a hot potato and demand they give the gifts back.[434] She eventually focused her attention on an impoverished young cleric with no apparent marital interest and gradually cut herself off from family completely.

Chapter 20

WEDDINGS WEST AND EAST

Meanwhile, since John had finally found a job, he and Lucy reached an "understanding," a prelude to an official engagement. Although Alice liked and respected Lucy as a person, she was concerned by the fact that Lucy had no religious affiliation, in contrast to her own family's strong religious background. She felt that a difference in background could potentially cause trouble in a marriage.[435] Nevertheless, the couple persevered. Lucy announced their official engagement to her friends and relations in California on May 4, 1935, at a party at her family's home in Walnut Creek as a surprise, in addition to the advertised reason for celebrating: her upcoming birthday on May 7.[436] The marriage was scheduled to take place in the garden of the home on August 21, 1935.

John, Alice, Louise and John's best friend and best man, Bob Follmer, flew out to California a few days in advance. John's uncle Harvey Wadham saw the group off at the airport. It was the day after Will Rogers and Wiley Post had died in a plane crash in Alaska, and he somberly wished them "Goodbye" as though he feared he might not see them again.

At that time, airline passengers' food was placed on trays set on pillows on their laps, and planes were not pressurized. Alice, in her black dress and veil, was sitting in front of Louise. The plane hit an air pocket going over the Rockies, and Louise's potato salad landed on her mother's veil. The turbulence made Louise sick as well. Unperturbed, Alice went in search of paper bags to deal with the situation. The lack of pressure in the cabin had bothered Alice, so John suggested she chew some gum to help reduce the effect. She chewed gum frantically all the rest of the way to San Francisco. When they got off the plane, her jaws hurt so much she couldn't talk.[437]

Lucy's mother was rather shocked to note Alice's size. She asked her daughter, "Why didn't you tell me?" to which she replied, "I just have never noticed it. I've known her these years, and I just never think of it. It just…she is."[438]

The wedding took place at 8:30 a.m. in the garden on August 21 as planned. In honor of the occasion, Alice wore a white print dress instead of her usual black. The Reverend Frederick Miller conducted the ceremony. Only members of the two families were present. The bride and groom left for a honeymoon trip up the Redwood Highway to the Columbia River.[439] They also planned to visit Yosemite.[440]

To give them a resounding sendoff, Lucy's brother Phillip welded a number of tin cans to the back axle of the honeymoon car. John and Lucy drove out to a happy clanging cacophony. As soon as they were a reasonable distance from the house, John got out of the car, clipped off the noisemakers and quietly left them in the ditch. When the couple came back from their trip, he stopped to retrieve and attach them again before returning to the house, startling his in-laws.

After the wedding, Alice and Louise went on a tour of the West and stopped over in Banff, Alberta. They stayed there a number of days, as Louise unfortunately had developed an infected pilonidal cyst at the base of her spine, making sitting very painful. A doctor lanced the cyst, but it took a while for her to recover, so she stayed in the hotel room while her mother went down for meals alone. Alice told the other guests her daughter was ill upstairs, and of course, they assumed she was tiny like her mother. After about a week, Louise felt well enough to go down for dinner with her, "both of us in our elegant evening gowns that we had worn at John and Lucy's wedding. We sashayed into the dining room, this tiny little lady with her great, huge, hulking daughter and the entire dining room almost fainted."[441]

Alice was inordinately proud of her big daughter and showed her off to surprise or even gently manipulate others on a number of different occasions. Louise was already taller than Alice by the time she was eleven or twelve. If they got on a subway car in New York and there was only one seat available, Alice would push her into the empty place, which embarrassed her. Then Alice would loudly say, "But I'm much more used to standing up, and I can hold myself better than you can." Before long, some man in the car would offer her his seat.[442]

When the Redfields returned home to Tenafly after the wedding, John and Lucy took up residence in one of the apartments in the house on Magnolia

Bridal party, John Redfield–Lucy Bancroft wedding, Walnut Creek, California. *From left to right*: Bob Follmer, John Redfield, Lucy Bancroft and Mary Jane Pollock. *Alice Irizarry.*

Alice Redfield in the midst of the wedding guests. *Alice Irizarry.*

Above: The decorated honeymoon car.
Alice Irizarry.

Left: Clarke and Dot Redfield at Atlantic City.
Nancy Carkhuff.

Street. But John's wedding was not the only one to occur in that year. Plans were already underway for Clarke's wedding as well.

Precisely how Clarke and his bride-to-be, Dorothy "Dot" Zabriskie, met and became engaged is unknown. Dot was six years younger than he was. Since her family lived on Engle Street near his parents' home, they may simply have become acquainted as neighbors. Meeting her helped him overcome the depression he felt after his father's death.[443] Still, he remained rather quiet and reserved.

They married on November 9, 1935, in the Episcopal Church of the Atonement in Tenafly. At the time, Clarke was working as an air conditioning engineer, when that concept was just being introduced. He subsequently went on to work for Wright Aeronautical, where he was in charge of determining what machine tools were needed for production. He continued there through World War II.[444]

Louise's romance proceeded quite differently. From the time she first became interested in boys, she had her eye on only one. Laurence "Larry" Levy sat across the room from her at chapel services, and she would wink at him when no one was looking. By the time they were in high school, they were dating. Her parents were quite strict. Even when she was a senior, she had to be home by ten o'clock at night. She felt this was rather unfair, as a freshman neighbor girl was allowed out until midnight.[445]

Larry, who was nine months younger than Louise, graduated from Tenafly High in 1934. The yearbook entry for him there, after listing his accomplishments, also noted his interest in a "certain blonde."[446] Unfortunately, in 1935, Larry suffered a severe bout of scarlet fever. It left him with some permanent damage to his heart that necessitated a long convalescence. Stanley Clarke and his wife knew Larry well, as he was a close friend of their son Dumont and came to visit him almost daily during that time.[447] Larry subsequently recovered and went on to earn a degree in engineering.

Larry's health situation—plus his Jewish-sounding surname—caused Alice some concern for her daughter's potential future happiness with him. Since significant anti-Jewish prejudice existed at the time, she worried that her daughter might have to face unpleasant discrimination as a result.

Most likely she also had in mind her own unfortunate experience with first love and wanted Louise to get to know other young men before deciding on a spouse. She finally told her that she couldn't marry Larry until she had received marriage proposals from at least seven other men first. Louise set out to meet the requirement. She persuaded one of Clarke's friends and a couple of her cousin Katherine Wadham's male relatives, among others, to propose, carefully choosing individuals she did not wish to marry and telling her mother of each proposal she received.[448]

Chapter 21

SETTLING DOWN

With the first two weddings over, Alice went back to dealing with other things. One of her friends, Mrs. Vanderberg, had recently been divorced, and in order to earn extra money to support herself, she became a travel agent. To help her out, Alice decided to send Louise and Ellery off with her on a trip to Europe. In addition to assisting the lady financially, that got Louise away from Larry, provided her another opportunity to meet other young men and left Alice herself with a free summer, "killing about three birds with one stone."[449]

She continued to help others out as well. One neighbor had been recently widowed. Alice loaned her the money to get started in the insurance business and introduced her to some of her friends so she could get going.[450] Another widowed friend, Mrs. Watson, found a job writing the social column for the local newspaper, and she would check with Alice regularly for family news to include.[451]

While Louise was studying at Goucher, the family of one of her college friends who lived in Baltimore had been wonderfully hospitable to her. The girl's father's coal business went broke during the Depression. In addition, he had served as a trustee of a bank, and the family had beggared itself trying to pay off every penny of the bank's obligations. Then the man died, leaving his family short of funds. One of the few things they had left were some Oriental rugs, so Alice, who didn't really need them, bought the rugs to help them out.[452]

John and Lucy Redfield's house, 18 Sisson Terrace, Tenafly. *Alice Irizarry.*

By early 1937, John and Lucy were expecting their first child. They decided it was time for them to purchase a home of their own. They found a house they liked for sale at 18 Sisson Terrace, only about two blocks away from where Alice lived. The previous owner had lost it to foreclosure, so they were able to obtain it at a favorable price.

Tragically, John and Lucy's first child was stillborn, and the doctors were not exactly sure why. Should they try to have another child of their own in the future? Might the same thing happen again? Should they consider adoption instead? After long and careful consideration, and with the best medical advice available, they decided that they would try again to have a child at a later date.

When Lucy told her parents of their decision, she received a thoughtful, supportive letter from her father in response. He assured her that if he had been in her position, he would have made the same decision. He added,

> *If by any chance there <u>should</u> be any unfortunate results, don't blame yourself or feel remorse. My whole philosophy of life is to try to do the very best I can, and then if the results are disappointing or unfortunate, as they*

are sometimes bound to be, I don't waste any time, strength, or power for future achievement in vain regrets or remorse. I am very glad you decided as you have, and I believe that after a normal amount of worrying Mother will be even more glad than I—that is after her grandchild arrives.[453]

That spring, Alice's curiosity was aroused by a newspaper article about handwriting analysis. A man offered to analyze handwriting samples from interested individuals and publish the results. To protect the subjects' anonymity, he would describe them only by their initials, presented in a scrambled order. Alice sent him a sample.

The published result reads as follows:

A.R.C.—Tenafly—You seem most curious, guarded and wary. Have you perhaps, at some time in your life been deceived in one whom you trusted? So that you now have no great amount of faith in human nature? The question is prompted by the mistrust that runs through your writing. It is so marked that it is unusual—going beyond the bounds of ordinary prudence, discretion or diplomacy.

Now I have encountered that before, and the writer was unaware that she tended to be mistrustful of people. One case in particular comes to mind. The writer vehemently denied this to be her general attitude but investigation on her part finally brought to light that in early childhood an incident had occurred that left an indelible imprint on her mind; not on her normal mind—that had forgotten, but on her subconscious which never forgets. You will best know if there is anything in this observation; I am only giving you the meaning of a sign that occurs in every line of your interesting letter.

And, as if to corroborate its truth, you have positive talent for telling nothing or nobody that which you judge best kept to yourself. Intimates possibly excepted. But even they are not encouraged to pry into your personal affairs and will learn nothing by attempting to pump you. Mentally you are sharp and keen, well educated—your brain never sleeps. You perceive without being told, know intuitively motive and intention and if not crossed have a really good disposition.

You are so hasty in whatever you do or say, however, that your pen doesn't seem to write fast as you think. While you may have an aggressive temperament, it seems to go with a reserved exterior and manner. Or is that your caution again, for you are naturally friendly, active, ambitious and energetic. Have splendid physical strength and endurance.

Your will-power is very strong; you are firm and didactic. What you set your mind to do, you will do. There is much determination in your hand, and contradiction—unless original and dramatic—does not interest you. You have all the initiative you need to put your plans through and are efficient and resourceful in deciding how to put in your time.

Culture is marked, good taste, liking for the best. A snappy entertaining talker, with dramatic instincts; clever and bright, a good mixer. Emotional, demonstrative, imaginative, adventurous and self-confident. You have a unique personality—no doubt are well liked.[454]

Impressed by the general accuracy of these observations, Alice saved the clipping.

John and Lucy and some friends got together and decided it would be fun to produce their own movies. John had received an 8-mm movie camera from Lucy as a wedding gift. Her maid of honor had given them a movie projector as well.[455] All they needed to do was decide on a script and assign the parts. *Little Red Riding Hood*, one of their productions, was staged in the backyard of their new home. The property was covered with trees, which served to make a fine forest for Little Red to walk through. For *Dracula*, they went to a nearby estate that featured an impressive tower for the vampire to lurk in and pounce out of to capture unsuspecting maidens.

Another project the pair came up with was to construct a glassed-in porch where their back patio used to be. Alice contributed financially to the effort and then made a point of ensuring that her other children received a similar financial benefit as well. She firmly believed in treating them all equally.[456]

Meanwhile, changes were occurring at the Redfield family property where Alice lived. In 1938, Clarke and Dot built themselves a small house there in the Cape Cod saltbox style a short distance north of Alice's house where the family orchard used to be.[457]

By early 1939, Dot and Lucy were both expecting. Clarke and Dot's daughter, Nancy Joan Redfield, was born on April 19, 1939. On September 10, 1939, Lucy gave birth to a healthy baby boy, much to everyone's relief. He was named Charles Eldred Redfield in honor of his maternal great-grandfather.[458] Lucy called him "Chuck" from the beginning to avoid the nickname "Charlie."

Alice adored her grandchildren. Since Nancy lived right next door, she would often run over to visit with her grandmother. She liked riding on the lawn swing in Alice's yard, and from time to time, the two of them would have a meal of bluefish and baked potatoes together.[459] Chuck's parents

John building the glassed-in porch on the house. *Alice Irizarry*.

threw a large party for family and friends on his first birthday, and Alice thoroughly enjoyed the event.

Finally, Alice concluded that she was not going to change Louise's mind about marrying Larry. Family and friends received copies of their engagement picture. A week before the wedding, Ellery asked to meet Larry for lunch, as he had something serious to tell him. He explained that his sister was a terrible slob and that he would find dirty clothes casually thrown into corners. He really shouldn't take a chance on her. Louise acknowledged that she was not a particularly tidy person. That did not deter Larry.

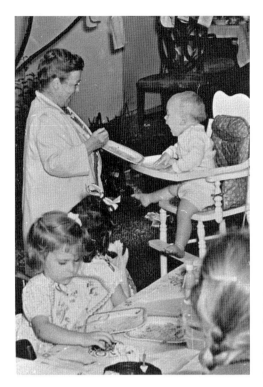

Left: Alice feeding her grandson Chuck at his first birthday party. *Author's collection.*

Below: Engagement photo of Louise Redfield and Laurence Levy. *Alice Irizarry.*

The wedding took place on November 11, 1939, in the living room of Alice's home. For their honeymoon trip, the couple went to New Orleans. Larry soon discovered Louise also lacked experience in cooking. On the first morning after their return from their honeymoon, they had to go to a dog wagon to get coffee, since she didn't know how to make it herself.[460]

For a while, almost every day after that she had to ask her mother how to prepare whatever she was planning to serve for dinner. On one memorable occasion she tried to make "chicken broilers" the way her mother did at home. They decided she should get the chicken, bring it to Alice's house and do the basic preparation there. What could go wrong? Louise took the prepared dish back home and placed it under the broiler. Before long, everything went up in flames. Despite the name, the chicken was supposed to have been baked, not broiled.[461]

Contrary to Alice's fears, the only overt discrimination Louise experienced as a result of her marriage was being ousted from the local golf club, something she didn't particularly miss.[462] Due to lingering uncertainties about Larry's health, the couple determined to do what they could while they could to enjoy their life together. The following year, they took an extended trip through the West and all through the Grand Canyon. The year after that, they went on a long trip to Mexico.[463]

Now that Louise had left home, Alice decided that she needed to learn how to drive a car herself. Her gardener-chauffeur was getting on in years, and looking after the property took up almost all his time. She had shied away from driving earlier because she felt it was too dangerous and worried about what would become of her children if something happened to her as a result.

Since her children were now all grown, she decided the time to learn had finally come, and she begged Louise to teach her. Every day at noon, she and Louise would drive down to a wide dead-end street that had been built for a development that never quite materialized near the border of Tenafly and Cresskill. Her car was specially equipped with a gearshift attached to the steering column. The pedals were raised so she could reach them with her feet. She sat up on cushions on the seat so that she could see out the windshield.

Her worst problem was trying to signal for a turn. If she put her hand out the window to indicate a left turn, she would pull to the right with her other hand on the wheel. Finally, they rigged a directional signal arrow that she could manage from where she sat. Alice eventually did learn to drive but remained rather terrified by the process.

Ellery Redfield and Eileen Eversley wedding. *Nancy Carkhuff.*

Nevertheless, determined to prove that she could successfully go anywhere she needed to be, she surprised Louise one afternoon by showing up at the home where she and Larry were living in Upper Montclair. To get there, she had to cross a number of bridges and successfully maneuver along a busy highway. Satisfied with the success of her venture, she did not stay long, as she wanted to get safely back home ahead of rush hour traffic.[464]

At Christmas, everyone gathered at Alice's house to celebrate the season. One year, as a surprise gift, Alice decided to hide a one hundred-dollar bill inside a walnut shell for each of her children and placed the innocent-looking walnuts in their Christmas stockings. Unfortunately, this ruse was not discovered until after two of the walnut shells had been tossed, unopened, into the fire.

On December 7, 1940, Ellery Redfield married Eileen Eversley, the girl he had landed in the pond with. He had a strong interest in flying, and by then, World War II was already raging in Europe. He took flight training so he would be ready if the United States decided to join the conflict.

In the spring of 1941, Lucy was expecting another child, and when she went to her doctor for her regular check-ups, each time he asked her for a blood sample. She could not understand why. The only reason she knew for frequent blood tests was to check for venereal disease. Finally, she confronted him, pointing out that she was "not that kind of woman." The doctor then explained that since her husband's blood type was Rh positive, and hers was Rh negative, he was checking to see whether she was developing antibodies to the child she was carrying, in case it too was Rh positive. As a result of recent research, he suspected such an occurrence might have caused the death of her first child. Fortunately, the blood tests showed that no antibodies were developing. Alden Redfield was born without problems on May 10, 1941.[465]

Chapter 22

REACHING THE END

Shortly after the United States declared war on December 7, 1941, Ellery enlisted in the U.S. Army Air Force, hoping to be sent overseas. Instead, because of his knowledge of flying, he was stationed in Florida to serve in a flight school to train others. When he came home on leave, he entertained the family with amusing anecdotes about his training experiences. Stanley's son Dumont joined the navy.

The other young men in the family did not serve. Clarke continued his work for Wright Aeronautical doing top-secret research for the military. His second child, Marcia Ann, was born on October 7, 1942.[466] John's lack of binocular vision and Larry's heart condition kept both of them out of military service.

By early 1942, Louise was expecting her first child. When she told Alice, she thought her mother would be thrilled. Instead, she burst out crying. "But Louise, that means the end of your youth! It's over! You've been having such a good time! It's been so good for Laurence! Are you sure you want to do this to him?"[467] Obviously, her earlier worries regarding her son-in-law had evaporated.

When Louise realized that the time for the birth had arrived, the first thing she did was wash her hair. She was determined to look right for the event. She called Larry, who came home from work after calling Alice, who joined them. They all sat around having afternoon tea until it was time to go to the hospital.

Little Louise Redfield Levy was born early on the morning of November 4, 1942. Then her mother, Louise, discovered that she could not nurse the baby and was most distressed. Alice visited her in the hospital and did her best to reassure her. She talked to her for a long time, explaining that some people could, and some people couldn't, and it might be best if she just fed the baby with a bottle. That way she could have better control of the process.[468]

What Alice did not tell her at the time was that she herself had just been diagnosed with breast cancer and needed to have a breast removed. She delayed dealing with the problem until Louise was home from the hospital and comfortably settled in with her new baby.

After her surgery and radiation treatment, Alice appeared to be doing well at first, but then it was discovered that the cancer had spread to her liver. Despite the bloating caused by her condition, she remained upbeat. On one of her visits to her doctor, she greeted him facetiously, "Well you don't have to tell me what I have! I'm pregnant! I'm having a baby!" That brought down the house and relieved the tension.[469]

When she knew she definitely had terminal cancer, she decided to get some things in order. She retrieved her jewelry from the safety-deposit box at the bank and selected which pieces to give to her daughter and to each of her daughters-in-law. She even set aside some to be given to the maids who had served her faithfully. She discussed with Clarke and John, who were to be executors of her will, what specifically she wanted done. She also reminded all her children that they could fight over the things in the house after she was dead. She was not going to say one word as to who was to get what.[470]

As Alice's condition worsened, Louise and Larry moved up to her house with her, as they had promised to do. They had a nurse there to help with her as well. She became quite unhappy and frustrated with being ill. Sometimes, Louise had to give her an enema. She hated needing to have her daughter do that for her. Louise reminded her that that was what had been called the "Redfield treatment" while the children had been growing up. Whenever they felt ill, she would administer an enema to them. Louise told her, "Mother, I'm getting back at you! You know you deserve it." Alice laughed at that, but she still hated it. The very last afternoon, she told the nurse, "Well, I just hope Louise isn't here, I'm such a mess!"[471]

Alice passed away on Friday May 7, 1943, at the age of sixty-six. The funeral service was held on Monday afternoon, May 10, 1943, at her home on Engle Street. Her brother-in-law, Harvey Wadham, senior deacon at Grace

TENAFLY, N. J., MAY 14, 1943   Subscription—$1.50 a Year / Issued Weekly   PRICE: THREE CENTS

Tenafly Pays Tribute To Mrs. Henry W. Redfield Prominent Civic Leader

Mrs. Henry Wells Redfield

A large number of relatives and friends joined in a final tribute to Mrs. Alice Coe Clarke Redfield, widow of the late Henry Wells Redfield, at funeral services Monday afternoon at her home on Engle Street, Tenafly. Mrs. Redfield, 66, who was well-known for her outstanding and charitable service in the community, passed away Friday night. She had been in failing health for several months.

Harvey N. Wadham, senior deacon at the Grace Chapel, of which Mrs. Redfield was a member, opened the service with prayer. Scriptures were read by the Rev. John H. Rosebaugh, rector of the Episcopal Church of the Atonement, Tenafly, and the Rev. Richard Hill, of Glen Cove, L. I. preached the sermon. Interment took place at the Brookside Cemetery Englewood.

Mrs. Redfield was born on July 23, 1876, the daughter of the late Dumont Clarke, Wall Street financier, and Cornelia Ellery
(Continued on Page 4)

Pays Tribute

(Continued from Page 1)
Clarke. The town of Dumont was named for her father who served there as Mayor.

Until recent days Mrs. Redfield continued her work in civic and welfare activities. She has been a resident of Tenafly for 37 years. She was a member of the Board of Managers of the Mary Fisher Home, a member of the Tenafly Civic Association, and annually donated the Henry W. Redfield Memorial Prize to pupils in Tenafly High School to commemorate the memory of her husband who died 12 years ago.

Her brothers and sisters are Lewis Latham Clarke, of New York; E. Stanley Clarke, former Mayor of Tenafly; The Rev. Dumont Clarke, of Nashville, Tenn.; Miss Corinne I. Clarke, of Demarest, and Mrs. George Case, of Englewood.

She is also survived by three sons, Clarke Redfield, John Alden Redfield, Frank Ellery Redfield, and a daughter, Mrs. Louise Redfield Levy, of Tenafly; also five grandchildren, Nancy Joan Redfield, Marcia Ann Redfield, Charles Eldred Redfield, Alden Redfield and Louise Redfield Levy, Jr.

—o—

"Tenafly Pays Tribute to Mrs. Henry W. Redfield, Prominent Civic Leader." *Northern Valley Tribune*, May 14, 1943. *Alice Irizarry.*

Chapel, gave the opening prayer. Scriptures were read by the Reverend John H. Rosebaugh, rector of the Episcopal Church of the Atonement in Tenafly. The Reverend Richard Hill of Glen Cove, Long Island, gave the sermon. She was laid to rest at the Brookside Cemetery in Englewood.

In addition to a front-page article about her, the *Northern Valley Tribune* ran an editorial calling her passing a great loss to Tenafly. The paper also included a letter in tribute from Mrs. Rosebaugh, and a resolution of appreciation from the Civic and Welfare Association.[472] Yet perhaps the greatest tribute she received was that in all the accolades, her size was never once mentioned. She was truly valued simply for the remarkable person that she had been.

Chapter 23

AFTERWARD

L ouise and Larry continued living in the Redfield family home. Alice's children had decided to delay the distribution of her effects until Ellery could get home on furlough from his military service, about six months after Alice's passing. On a Sunday afternoon, Louise and Larry set out all the family silver, china and such on the dining room table for viewing. Alice's children and their spouses then retired to the living room for a round of drinks, during which Louise reviewed the various items elsewhere in the house for them. Next, she made sure everyone had a pad and pen. They then went through the house making notes on what items were of interest to each of them.

They had decided that selections would be made one item at a time following the birth order of the siblings. Clarke made his choice first. John made his second. Both took items of sentimental value. When Louise's turn came, much to the surprise of the others, she took the house. While that choice was unexpected, they decided to let it stand. Selections continued until everyone had all they wanted. Sometimes, more than one person wanted an item, but birth order selection determined the result.[473]

Although Alice had lived to see many of her grandchildren, more were born after her death. Laurence M. Levy Jr. was born on August 23, 1945. On January 13, 1946, John and Lucy had a daughter they named Alice in her honor. Her blood type was Rh positive, but with careful monitoring, the doctor was able to deliver her before her mother's body produced a dangerous level of harmful antibodies. Tragically, young Alice died of SIDS at the age of three months. Ellery and Eileen's son William was born on October 22, 1947.[474]

Living so close to one another, Clarke's, John's and Louise's families got together frequently, and their children spent a lot of time together while they were growing up. They all thoroughly enjoyed the playroom with its stage, cork floor and dumbwaiter as their parents had done before them in the house that Henry had designed. Some of the other features were less convenient. When the Levys took possession of the house, Larry had all the sinks raised to their normal height, although he did not raise the doorknobs as well.[475] Ellery and his family lived a couple of towns away and only joined the others rarely for special events like Christmas and Easter.

Despite their parents' strong religious beliefs, none of Alice's children followed precisely in their footsteps. John and his two sons attended the morning Lord's Supper services at the chapel regularly. Lucy did not go with them. John also served as secretary and treasurer for the chapel for many years. Although he smoked regularly at home, he left his cigarettes behind when he attended services. Louise and her family went to chapel occasionally, but not on a regular basis. Clarke and Ellery and their families rarely attended.

After the war, Clarke and Larry both went to work with the Bendix Corporation for a number of years. John continued at Bankers Trust in various positions. He ended up in the personnel department, matching employees with their supervisors and working to solve any difficulties that might arise. Ellery worked at a variety of different jobs, both in aviation and as a salesman.

Stanley's son Dumont left the navy and went to work for Imperial Oil. Before the war, he had run the service station on Tenafly, so he started with some knowledge of the oil business. After spending a number of years at various posts abroad in the Near East and Europe, he rose to become a major marketing executive for the company.[476] He and Larry remained close friends.

Alice's short siblings lived to ripe old ages. Stanley passed away from a heart attack in 1961 at the age of ninety-one. After spending a number of years in a nursing home due to Alzheimer–like symptoms, Corinne died in 1975 at age ninety-four. Sadly, her self-absorption and waspish tongue had left her virtually isolated from her family and former friends.

There wasn't a street along the east side of the Redfield property when Henry purchased it, nor was one developed there prior to World War I. After the war, however, a new street called Grand View Terrace was opened up, running north from Highwood Avenue and continuing along and past the property's eastern edge.

Like many other towns and cities, Tenafly also experienced a postwar expansion and building boom following World War II. In 1952, the western half of the Redfield property facing on Engle Street was divided into two lots and sold. About that same time, the house that Henry had built for Alice received a new address, 25 Grand View Terrace.

In 1976, the Levys sold Alice's house and moved to a smaller residence in Demarest. Clarke passed away in 1972. Following the passing of his wife, Dorothy, in 1983, their house was sold to a family that wanted a much larger residence. The main portion of the structure was torn down and replaced, but the front entry was retained. By doing that, the new owners were able to claim the work as remodeling for tax purposes. The house that Henry built for Alice still stands today.

Chapter 24

WHY WAS ALICE SHORT?

During Alice's lifetime, the cause of her abnormal shortness and that of her two short siblings was unknown. However, their size clearly meets the medical standard for dwarfism, an adult height of less than four feet, ten inches. With the development of genetic studies, it is possible to make a good guess as to the reason for their condition. It appears to have been a form of pituitary dwarfism. In about two-thirds of such cases, there is a complete failure in the production of all pituitary hormones, including those that lead to sexual maturity. Individuals so affected and untreated would not only be abnormally short but also be unable to have children. The remaining third of pituitary dwarves suffer from some form of isolated growth hormone deficiency, in which only their height is affected. This condition is quite rare, estimated to occur in only one in about four thousand to ten thousand individuals worldwide.[477]

Since their parents and their other siblings all grew to normal size, it appears that Alice and her short siblings suffered from a recessive genetic condition. Their parents both happened to carry the same mutated recessive gene on one of the two chromosomes that form one of the twenty-three pairs found in normal human cells.

Twenty-two of these pairs are termed autosomes. When a recessive mutated gene is on one of a pair of autosomes, the normal gene on the other member of the pair masks the effect of the abnormal one, and the individual appears normal. Since each child gets half of each pair of its chromosomes from each parent, three different genetic results are possible

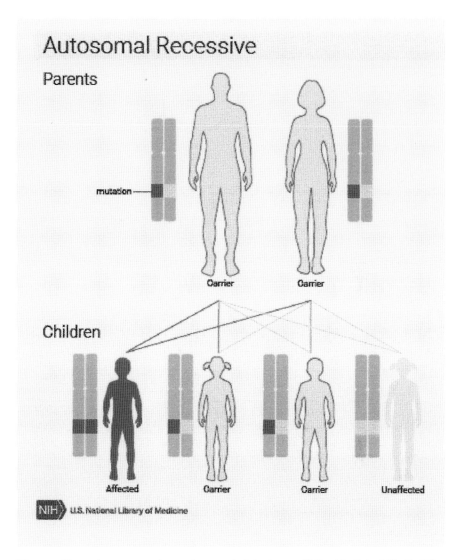

Diagram illustrating autosomal recessive genetic inheritance. *National Institute of Health, U.S. Library of Medicine.*

for the parents' offspring if both are carriers of the mutation. Statistically, one quarter of them will receive two normal chromosomes and not carry the trait. One quarter of them will receive two abnormal chromosomes and exhibit the trait as a result. The remaining half of them will receive a normal chromosome from one parent and an abnormal one from the other and will thus appear normal but be carriers of the trait.

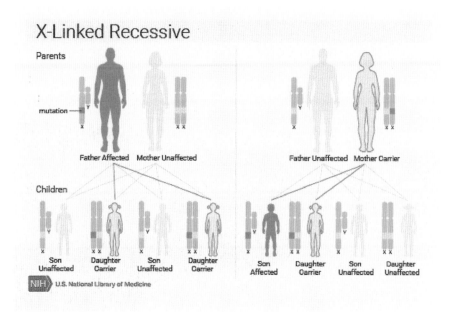

Diagram illustrating X-linked genetic inheritance. *National Institute of Health, U.S. Library of Medicine.*

The final pair of chromosomes is the sex chromosomes, two X chromosomes in a woman, or an X and a Y chromosome in a man. If a recessive mutation is present on only one of the X chromosomes in a woman, the normal gene on the other X chromosome will mask it, and the individual will appear normal. However, if the mutation is on the X chromosome of the man, due to his shorter Y chromosome not fully matching the X, he will show the trait. Thus, mutations on the X chromosome are termed sex-linked mutations.

Since Alice and her short siblings all developed normally in all other respects, it appears that their shortness was due to some type of isolated growth hormone deficiency. Four different forms of isolated growth hormone deficiency have been identified, each with a different genetic component. These are classified as Type 1A, Type 1B, Type II and Type III.[478]

Types 1A and 1B are inherited in an autosomal recessive pattern. They may be caused by either a mutation of the gene for the production of growth hormone (GH1) or the gene for the growth hormone–releasing hormone receptor (GHRHR). The receptor attaches to a molecule called the growth hormone–releasing hormone. The binding of GHRHR to the

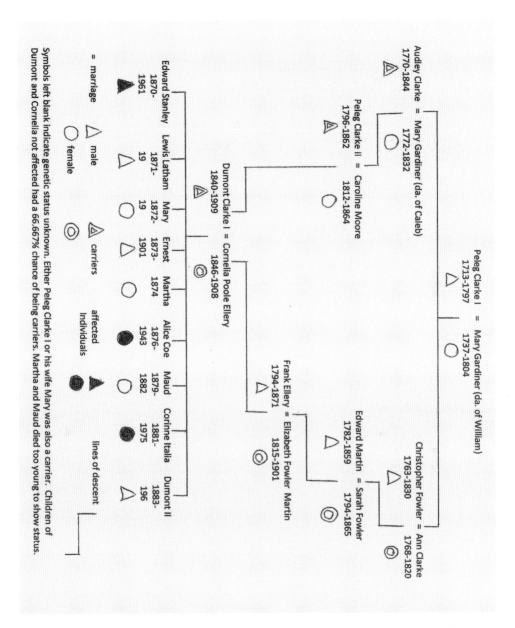

Diagram showing the relationship between Dumont Clarke and Cornelia Ellery. *Judy Redfield.*

receptor triggers the production of the growth hormone and its release from the pituitary gland.

Type 1A is the result of the absence of growth hormone and is the most severe type. This condition can be noted at birth, as affected infants are shorter than normal.

Individuals with Type 1B produce very low levels of growth hormone. Although short, such individuals are not as short as those with Type 1A. Their condition usually becomes apparent in early to mid-childhood.

Type II, on the other hand, also a mutation of the GH1 gene, is inherited in a dominant pattern. A single copy of the gene from one parent is sufficient to cause the condition. It can also be the result of a new mutation when there is no history of the condition in the family.

Type III is inherited in an X chromosome–related pattern caused by mutations in the BTK gene. However, it is unknown how mutations in this gene contribute to growth hormone deficiency. Affected fathers cannot pass on such X-linked conditions to their sons, as they give them a Y chromosome, not an X.

Which type best matches the condition of Alice and her short siblings? The fact that their condition was clearly a recessive one eliminates Type II. The fact that Stanley's father, Dumont, did not exhibit the trait eliminates Type III. None of the available information suggests that Alice and her short siblings were abnormally short at birth, making Type 1A unlikely. Thus the cause of the shortness of Alice and her siblings appears most likely to be the result of a Type 1B isolated growth hormone deficiency. Since their condition was both rare and recessive, the most likely reason for its appearance seems to be that their parents were related in some fashion.

Such indeed was the case. One set of Dumont Clarke's great-grandparents and one set of Cornelia Ellery's great-great grandparents were one and the same. Given the relationship, it is possible to deduce with reasonable certainty which of many of their ancestors were carriers of the trait, although it is not possible to determine which one of their two common ancestors was a carrier. Likewise, it is not possible to determine which of their normal-sized children were carriers and which were not.

Stanley's son and all of Alice's children were carriers for the trait, as they could receive only an abnormal gene from their short parent, along with the normal one they received from their parent of regular size. Their children each had a 50 percent chance of being carriers as well. If their grandchildren did, in fact, inherit the abnormal gene from their parents, then these children would likewise have a 50 percent chance of passing it on.

Charles Stratton wearing a beard, accompanied by Lavinia Warren. *Author's collection.*

At least some of the famous proportional dwarves mentioned in the introduction to this book appear to have had a condition similar to Alice's. Although Lavinia Warren apparently did not attempt to have children, her dwarf sister Minnie Warren did. In 1877, Minnie Warren married Edmund Newell, another one of Barnum's short performers, described as "not quite a dwarf."[479] Not long after their marriage, she became pregnant—unfortunately, prior to the development of safe cesarean procedures. When her child was due to be born, because of her small size, she was unable to deliver it, and both she and the infant died.[480]

Count Boruwlaski was one of three proportional dwarves in his family, two boys and a girl.[481] He married a woman of normal size, and they had three and possibly four daughters together.[482]

The situation is less clear with regard to Charles Stratton, General Tom Thumb. In a number of photos, Charles Stratton is shown with a mustache or a beard, secondary sexual characteristics that would appear to indicate that he was sexually mature. For a long time, many physicians did not realize that some proportionate dwarves could be sexually mature, as individuals with total pituitary hormone failure were much more common. They suggested that the various mustaches and beards that he wore were false. Obviously, there is no way to know for sure at this point.

Not a great deal of information is available on Jeremy Hudson. There is no record of him having married, although he is supposed to have had a mistress at one point.

Some other medical conditions mentioned earlier in the text also have genetic causes. Hemophilia, which results from a lack of sufficient clotting proteins in the blood, is usually the result of an X chromosome–linked recessive condition. As a result, affected individuals tend to bleed excessively from injuries, at times to a life-threatening degree. Mary Clarke Case was most likely a carrier for the gene, which she passed on to her son Robert, who suffered from it.

The blood type incompatibility between John Redfield and his wife, Lucy, is the result of an autosomal condition. The Rh positive condition is a dominant one, while the Rh negative condition is recessive. Lucy's blood type was Rh negative. John's was Rh positive. However, he was obviously a carrier for the Rh negative condition, as his two sons, Chuck and Alden, both were Rh negative.

TAKEAWAYS

I n presenting Alice's story, I have purposely done so in an essentially narrative style, rather than attempting a detailed analytical approach. At the same time, I trust I have provided enough detail that should anyone wish to follow that route there is ample information for them to do so.

In many ways, the lives of Alice and her family provide a distinct contrast to those of other proportional dwarves for whom detailed biographies exist. Unlike some, Alice was not the only dwarf in her family. Like Joseph Boruwlaski and Lavinia Warren, she had dwarf siblings.

However, unlike all of the others mentioned in the text, financial needs or desires were not a significant issue in determining the individual lifestyles of Alice and her short siblings. Nor were they regarded as strange and subject to special treatment due to their size within their family. In addition, since they lived in the same general area virtually all of their lives, they were well known to their neighbors and accepted as part of the community. While they recognized that they differed in size from most other people, they nevertheless believed they could live essentially normal lives like their neighbors and friends. At least, Alice and Stanley certainly did so and set out to do precisely that. Their warm, outgoing personalities helped them to succeed.

Corinne, in contrast, while having the same background advantages, apparently had a much more self-focused and self-centered approach to life. She considered her condition a significant affliction. When her short siblings left the family to pursue their own lives and succeeded, she felt betrayed and abandoned by them and lashed out in response. Even in her later years, she appeared to lack self-confidence, attempting to buy friendship with gifts to others, then lashing out against them in turn when they developed additional friendships and interests. She ended up virtually alone, her own worst enemy.

Other things being equal, for the Clarke dwarves, facing adversity and working through it proved a much more rewarding and fulfilling life strategy than retreating into feeling sorry for themselves, a principle we should all keep in mind.

INDIVIDUALS INTERVIEWED

The majority of the interviews were conducted between February 27, 1980, and March 3, 1980, by Judy Redfield. Some individuals were interviewed more than once, the different interviews labelled sequentially with Roman numerals. Two additional interviews of John Redfield were conducted by Alden Redfield on December 26, 1981. The interviewees were:

Dumont Clarke III, the only surviving child of E. Stanley Clarke, the eldest brother of Alice Clarke Redfield, who, like Alice, was short.

Laurence Levy, husband of Louise Redfield Levy.

Louise Redfield Levy, only daughter and third child of Alice Clarke Redfield and Henry Wells Redfield Jr., the wife of Laurence Levy.

Katherine Stillman Neandross, next-door neighbor of the Redfields while Alice's children were growing up. Her mother, Elizabeth "Lizzie" Worth Stillman, had been a next-door neighbor and close friend of Alice while they were growing up. Katherine's father, Walter Stillman, was a close friend of Henry Redfield Jr.

Dorothy Redfield, wife of Clarke Redfield, eldest son of Alice Clarke Redfield and Henry Wells Redfield Jr. Clarke died in 1972.

John Alden Redfield, second son of Alice Clarke Redfield and Henry Wells Redfield Jr.

Frances Raymond, Alice Clarke Redfield's second cousin, the daughter of Jessie Clarke Raymond, Alice's cousin and close friend.

Katherine Wadham Swann, Alice's niece and a nearby neighbor of the Redfields while Alice's children were growing up. Her mother, Katherine "Kitty" Redfield Wadham, was Henry Redfield Jr.'s youngest sister. Her father, Harvey Wadham, along with Henry Wells Redfield Sr., was a founder of the evangelical group of Plymouth Brethren that became Grace Chapel in Tenafly.

NOTES

Introduction

1. Page, *Lord Minimus*, 2.
2. Grzeskowiak-Krwawicz, *Gulliver in the Land of Giants*, 96.
3. Sullivan, *Tom Thumb*, 102.
4. Grzeskowiak-Krwawicz, *Gulliver in the Land of Giants*, 91.
5. Sullivan, *Tom Thumb*, 182.
6. Ibid., 182–84.

1. All in the Family

7. Raymond, interview, 8.
8. Louise Redfield, "Behind the Headlines," 3.
9. Morrison, *Clarke Families of Rhode Island*, 240.
10. Rhode Island Deaths and Burials, 1802–1950, 66, public record.
11. *New York Commercial*, "A Type of the Successful New Yorker—Dumont Clarke," April 4, 1902.
12. Raymond, interview, 1.
13. Ellery, letter. This is a handwritten copy of a letter to an unidentified historian outlining Ellery genealogical data.
14. *New York Commercial*, "A Type of Successful New Yorker—Dumont Clarke," April 4, 1902.
15. Louise Redfield, "Behind the Headlines," 2.
16. Altschuler, *Dumont Heritage*, 75.

17. Morrison, *Clarke Families of Rhode Island*, 240.
18. *New York Times*, "Many Changes at National Banks," January 10, 1894.
19. Louise Redfield, "Behind the Headlines," 4.
20. *New York Times*, "Death of George S. Coe," May 4, 1896.
21. Louise Redfield, "Behind the Headlines," 5.
22. Altschuler, *Dumont Heritage*, 88.
23. Louise Redfield Levy, interview II, 23.
24. Dumont Clarke III, interview, 3.
25. *New York Commercial*, "A Type of Successful New Yorker—Dumont Clarke," April 4, 1902.
26. Raymond, interview, 3.
27. Ibid.
28. Louise Redfield, "Behind the Headlines," 5–6.
29. Ibid., 4–5.
30. Raymond, interview, 9.
31. Ibid., 23.
32. John A. Redfield, interview II, 4.
33. Louise Levy, interview II, 22.
34. John A. Redfield, interview II, 4.
35. Raymond, interview, 10.
36. Ernest Clarke, letter to Alice Clarke, October 5, 1896.
37. Alice Clarke and Fanny Clarke, letter to Cornelia Clarke, August 14, 1886.
38. Stanley Clarke, letter to Alice Clarke, February 16, 1890.
39. Unidentified newspaper clipping, "Lewis L. Clarke Takes Father's Post in Bank," January 12, 1910.
40. Cornelia Clarke, letter to Alice Clarke, May 16, 1893.

2. Growing Up Alice

41. Louise Levy, interview I, 1.
42. Raymond, interview, 1.
43. Ibid., 18.
44. Louise Levy, interview II, 22.
45. Ernest Clarke, letters to Alice Clarke, October 5, 1896, and November 2, 1896.
46. Louise Levy, interview II, 22.
47. Bordentown Female College, postcard, undated. Author's collection.
48. Bordentown Female College, tuition bill, 1864. Author's collection.
49. Raymond, interview, 2–3.

50. Ibid., 2.
51. Ibid., 3.
52. Wikipedia, "Dwight-Englewood School."
53. Dwight School report cards, 1894–95, for Alice Redfield.
54. Unidentified publication, Dwight School magazine advertisement, early 1900s.
55. Dwight School report cards.
56. John Redfield, II, 1–2
57. Louise Levy, interview I, 19.
58. John Redfield, interview II, 1.
59. Louise Levy, interview I, 2–3.
60. Ibid., 1.
61. Ibid.
62. Woodward, letters to Alice Redfield, December 1, 1895, and December 15, 1895.
63. Alice Clarke, diary, March 5, 1902.

3. The Kirksville Adventure

64. Trowbridge, *Andrew Taylor Still*, preface, xi–xii.
65. Ibid., 145
66. Ibid., 143.
67. Ibid., 149–51.
68. Ibid., 149.
69. Louise Levy, interview I, 1.
70. Alice Clarke, diary, January 16, 1902.
71. Alice Clarke, European trip diary, June 29, 1903.

4. Back Home

72. Altschuler, *Dumont Heritage*, 90.
73. Ibid., 91.
74. U.S. Census, 1900.
75. Unidentified newspaper clipping, "Lewis L. Clarke Takes Father's Post in Bank," January 12, 1910.
76. Cornelia Clarke, letter to Alice Clarke, March 3, 1893.
77. Ernest Clarke, letters to Alice Clarke, October 5, 1896, and November 2, 1896.
78. Alice Clarke, diary, multiple entries, 1900 and 1902.
79. Ibid., September 2, 1900.

80. Ibid., February 24, 1902, and April 26, 1902.
81. Ibid., multiple entries, 1900 and 1902.

5. Romance Begins to Bloom

82. Unidentified newspaper clipping, "Wedding Bells Redfield-Dakin," October 20, 1897.
83. *New York Times*, "Case-Clarke," March 13, 1898
84. Raymond, interview, 20.
85. *New York Times*, "Case-Clarke."
86. Raymond, interview, 20.
87. Morrison, *Clarke Families of Rhode Island*, 240.
88. Case, letter to Alice Clarke, November 4, 1897.
89. Case, letter to Alice Clarke, October 28, 1897.
90. Alice Clarke, diary, 1900, back flyleaf.
91. Louise Levy, interview I, 2.
92. Rigney and Stefanowicz, *Tenafly*, 69.
93. John Redfield, Interview II, 5
94. Alice Clarke, diary, June 20, 1900, and June 21, 1900.
95. Ibid., multiple entries, 1902.
96. Ibid., multiple entries, 1900.
97. Raymond, interview, 21–22.
98. Morrison, *Clarke Families of Rhode Island*, 241.
99. Ibid.
100. Raymond, letter to Alice Clarke, July 20, 1901.
101. Unidentified newspaper, "Human Caravan, Gold Laden, Halts Traffic in Broadway Near Cedar St. Twice Daily," 1899.

6. An Eventful Few Months

102. Alice Clarke, diary, February 7, 1902, and April 1, 1902.
103. Ibid., March 19, 1902.
104. *New York Times*, "Dumont Clarke Sells the *Tranquilo*," May 9, 1903.
105. *New York Commercial*, "A Type of Successful New Yorker—Dumont Clarke," April 4, 1902.
106. Dumont Clarke, Last Will and Testament, May 9, 1902.
107. Alice Clarke, diary, April 9, 1902.
108. Altschuler, *Dumont Heritage*, 98.
109. Alice Clarke, diary, May 15, 1902, and May 16, 1902.

110. Ibid., May 22, 1902.
111. Ibid., June 13, 1902.
112. Ibid., June 21, 1902.
113. Ibid., June 29, 1902.
114. Ibid., July 4, 1902.
115. Louise Levy, interview II, 17.
116. Alice Clarke, diary, July 20, 1902.
117. Ibid., August 4, 1902.
118. Ibid., August 5, 1902, and August 10, 1902.
119. Ibid., August 11–19, 1902.

7. Who Was that Young Man?

120. Richard Redfield, letter to Susan Jane Lowerre, August 31, 1843.
121. Note on the reverse of a picture of Richard W. Redfield, undated.
122. U.S. Census, 1850.
123. U.S. Census, 1860.
124. John Redfield, interview III, 19.
125. New York State Census, 1865.
126. U.S. Census, 1870.
127. Swann, interview, 14.
128. U.S. Census, 1880.
129. Swann, interview 6
130. Wikipedia, "Plymouth Brethren."
131. Swann, interview, 7.
132. Andrews, *Tenafly Public Library*, 4.
133. Rigney and Stefanowicz, *Tenafly*, 28.
134. Henry W. Redfield Sr., letter to his daughter Louise, September 29, 1880.
135. Swann, interview, 14.
136. John Redfield, interview I, 8.
137. John Redfield, interview III, 16–17.

8. A Fly in the Ointment

138. Alice Clarke, diary, September 2, 1902.
139. Speert, *Sloan Hospital Chronicle*, 125.
140. Cragin, "Sloan Hospital for Women," 5–8.
141. Speert, *Sloan Hospital Chronicle*, 127.
142. Ibid.

143. Thoms, *Our Obstetric Herit*age, 85.
144. Alice Clarke, diary, September 15, 1902.
145. Ibid., September 18, 1902.
146. Henry Redfield Jr., letter to Alice Clarke, September 19, 1902.
147. Ibid., September 23, 1902.
148. Alice Clarke, diary October 8, 1902.
149. Ibid., November 5, 1902.
150. Ibid., November 12, 1902.
151. Ibid., November 19, 1902.

9. The Grand Tour

152. *New York Times*, "Dumont Clarke Buys the Yacht *Kalolah*," May 13, 1903.
153. Alice Clarke, European trip diary, June 6, 1903.
154. Ibid., June 9, 1903.
155. Ibid., June 8, 1903, and June 16, 1903.
156. Ibid., June 10, 1903.
157. Ibid., June 21, 1903.
158. Ibid., July 3, 1903.
159. Wikipedia, "Heidelberg Tun."
160. Alice Clarke, European trip diary, July 6, 1903.
161. Ibid., July 14, 1903.
162. Ibid., July 16, 1903.
163. Ibid., July 17, 1903.
164. Ibid., July 27, 1903.
165. Cabois, letter to Alice Clarke, September 17, 1903.
166. Dumont Clarke, Last Will and Testament, September 5, 1902; First Codicil, September 15, 1903.

10. Tying the Knot

167. *Tenafly Record*, "Redfield-Clarke," January 23, 1904.
168. State of New Jersey marriage certificate, Henry W. Redfield Jr. and Alice Coe Clarke, January 20, 1904.
169. Henry Redfield, letter to Alice Clarke, January 19, 1904.
170. *Tenafly Record*, "Redfield-Clarke," January 23, 1904.
171. Wikipedia, "Lakewood Township."
172. *New York Herald*, "Lakewood's Tiniest Bride," January 23, 1904.
173. Corinne Clarke, letter to Alice and Henry Redfield, January 21, 1904.
174. *Tenafly Record*, "Redfield-Clarke," January 23, 1904.

175. Cornelia Clarke, letter to Alice Redfield, January 24, 1904.
176. Ibid.
177. Lavinia Redfield, letter to Henry Redfield Jr., January 24, 1904.
178. Corinne Clarke, letter to Alice and Henry Redfield, January 21, 1904.
179. Cornelia Clarke, letter to Alice Redfield, January 24, 1904.
180. U.S. Census 1930.
181. John Redfield, interview III, 23.
182. Ibid.
183. Cornelia Clarke, letter to Alice Redfield, January 24, 1904.
184. *New York Times*, "Ex-Mayor Low's Yacht Sold," April 2, 1904.
185. John Redfield, note, undated.
186. Louise Levy, interview I, 7–8.

11. Dreams Fulfilled

187. Cornelia Clarke, letter to Alice Redfield, July 22, 1906.
188. Dumont Clarke Jr., letter to Alice Redfield, August 3, 1906
189. Cragin, "Cesarean Section," 13.
190. Clarke Redfield's Baby Book, untitled page, September 11, 1909.
191. Cragin, "Treatment of Ectopic Gestation," 74
192. Neandross, interview, 5.
193. Cragin, "Sloan Hospital for Women," photo insert facing page 9.
194. Clarke Redfield's Baby Book, Height to Five Years page
195. *Tenafly Record*, March 30, 1907.
196. Sloan Hospital, "Recommended Infant Feeding List," 1907.
197. Clarke Redfield, baptismal certificate, July 23, 1907.
198. Clarke Redfield's Baby Book, Interesting Records page.
199. Rigney, *Tenafly's Unidentified Photographer*, 4.
200. Dumont Clarke Jr., letter to Alice Redfield, August 21, 1906.
201. Dumont Clarke Jr. U.S. passport application, January 19, 1907.
202. Dumont Clarke Jr., letter, "Work of the Y.M.C.A.," 1907.
203. Dumont Clarke Jr., letter, December 24, 1907.
204. Dumont Clarke Jr., letter, "Diseases of Southern India," March 12, 1908.
205. Ibid.

12. A Time of Loss and Change

206. *New York Times*, "Mrs. Dumont Clarke Dead," March 16, 1908.
207. John Redfield, interview II, 3.

208. Dumont Clarke Sr., Last Will and Testament of Dumont Clarke; Second Codicil, January 29, 1909.

209. Dumont Clarke Sr., letters to Alice Redfield, September 20, 1909, and October 25, 1909.

210. Clarke Redfield's Baby Book, untitled page, note dated September 11, 1909.

211. John Redfield's Baby Book, Baby's First Journey, note dated October 13, 1909.

212. Dumont Clarke Sr., letter to Alice Redfield, October 25, 1909.

213. John Redfield's Baby Book, untitled page, notes dated December 11, 1909, January 8, 1910, and October 26, 1910.

214. Swann, interview, 21.

215. Ibid.

216. Neandross, interview, 2.

217. Alice Clarke, diary, 1900 and 1902, multiple entries.

218. Neandross, interview, 3.

219. John Redfield, interview II, 24; Raymond, interview, 6; Swann, interview, 21.

220. *New York Times*, "Dumont Clarke Dies at 69, of Pneumonia," December 27, 1909.

221. Altschuler, *Dumont Heritage*, 97.

222. Unidentified newspaper clipping, "Lewis L. Clarke Takes Father's Post at Bank," January 12, 1910.

223. Altschuler, *Dumont Heritage*, 98.

224. Raymond, interview, 15.

225. Dumont Clarke Jr., letter to Alice Redfield, March 14, 1910.

226. *New York Times*, "Dumont Clarke a Pastor," January 1, 1911.

227. Ager, *We Plow God's Fields*, 107–9.

228. Raymond, interview, 14–15.

229. Dumont Clarke III, interview, 3.

13. Remodeling the Family Home

230. John Redfield, interview III, 16–17.

231. Swann, interview, 18.

232. Rigney and Stefanowicz, *Tenafly*, 80.

233. John Redfield, interview I, 12.

234. Louise Levy, interview I, 13

235. Ibid., 8.

236. John Redfield, interview I, 12.

237. Louise Levy, interview I, 13.
238. Laurence Levy, interview, 12.
239. Louise Levy, interview I, 14–15.
240. Ibid., 14.
241. Laurence Levy, interview, 15.

14. The Boys' Early Life

242. Clarke Redfield's Baby Book, unidentified page.
243. John Redfield's Baby Book, Notes page.
244. Clarke Redfield's Baby Book, unidentified page.
245. Neandross, interview, 12.
246. Ibid., 4.
247. Swann, interview, 2–3.
248. Ibid., 12–13.
249. Ibid., 2.
250. John Redfield, interview I, 18–19.
251. Neandross, interview, 2.
252. Louise Levy, interview II, 1.
253. Swann, interview, 7.
254. Dumont Clarke III, interview, 15.
255. Neandross, interview, 9; John Redfield, interview II, 6.
256. Dumont Clarke III, interview, 4.
257. Swann, interview, 11.
258. John Redfield's Baby Book, Baby's First Lesson, September ??, 1911.
259. Swann, interview, 11–12.
260. Ibid., 4.
261. John Redfield, interview III, 2.
262. Neandross, interview, 3.
263. Swann, interview, 4.
264. Ibid., 2.
265. Louise Levy, interview II, 6–7.

15. Wartime and Camp Merritt

266. Wikipedia, "United States in World War I."
267. Ager, *We Plow God's Fields*, 203.
268. John Redfield's Baby Book, Baby's First Journey.
269. Sloan Hospital for Women, Infant Patient Record for Louise Redfield, May 1, 1915.

270. Louise Redfield, letter to Alice Redfield, May 5, 1915.

271. Boroughs Nature Club membership certificates, inserted in John Redfield's Baby Book, December 1, 1916.

272. John Redfield's Baby Book, Baby's First Journey.

273. John Redfield, genealogical notes, n.d.

274. Wikipedia, "United States in World War I."

275. Souvenir folder of Camp Dodge, Des Moines, Iowa, circa 1917.

276. Bartholf, Camp Merritt, 7.

277. *Camp Merritt*, booklet prepared for monument dedication on May 30, 1924, 8.

278. Altschuler, *Dumont Heritage*, 104.

279. Merritt Hall, pamphlet, 2.

280. The Historian, "The Story of the U.S.A. Base Hospital at Camp Merritt, N.J." Pt. 1, *The Mess Kit* 1 no. 1 (March 1919): 10.

281. Ibid., 8–10.

282. Dumont Clarke III, interview, 1.

283. The Historian, "The Story of the U.S.A. Base Hospital at Camp Merritt, N.J." Pt. 2, *The Mess Kit* 1 no. 2 (April 1919): 10.

284. *Camp Merritt*, 12.

285. Ibid., 8–9.

286. Ibid., 14–15.

287. *Camp Merritt the Camp Beautiful*, information booklet for soldiers, 11.

288. John Redfield, interview II, 23.

289. *Camp Merritt*, 8–9.

290. *Merritt Hall*, 5–15.

291. *Camp Merritt the Camp Beautiful*, 8.

292. *Camp Merritt*, 16–17.

293. Ibid., 18.

294. Ibid., 19–20.

295. Ibid., 22-31.

296. John Redfield, interview III, 3.

297. Henry Redfield, Draft Registration Card, September 12, 1918.

298. John Redfield, interview II, 23.

299. Louise Levy, interview I, 20–21.

300. *Bergen County Record*, "Tenafly Council Meeting," January 5, 1918.

301. *Camp Merritt the Camp Beautiful*, 1.

302. Louise Levy, interview II, 16.

303. Dumont Clarke III, interview, 9–10.

16. Readjusting

304. Altschuler, *Dumont Heritage*, 106.
305. *Camp Merritt*, 43.
306. Ibid., 45.
307. Dumont Clarke III, interview, 10–11.
308. Louise Levy, interview II, 17.
309. John Redfield, interview III, 17.
310. John Redfield, interview I, 12.
311. Louise Levy, interview I, 22.
312. John Redfield, interview I, 11.
313. Rigney and Stefanowicz, *Tenafly*, 49.
314. John Redfield, interview II, 22.
315. Rigney and Stefanowicz, *Tenafly*, 49.
316. Swann, interview, 20.
317. Louise Levy, interview I, 10.
318. Laurence Levy, interview, 10.
319. Swann, interview, 24.
320. Neandross, interview, 1.
321. Dumont Clarke III, interview, 6.
322. Louise Levy, interview II, 17.
323. Raymond, interview, 22.
324. Dumont Clarke III, interview, 7.

17. Redfield Family Life in the 1920s

325. Swann, interview, 22.
326. John Redfield, interview I, 14.
327. Louise Levy, interview I, 8.
328. John Redfield, interview I, 6.
329. John Redfield, interview II, 12.
330. Louise Levy, interview I, 9.
331. John Redfield, interview II, 14.
332. Louise Levy, interview I, 10.
333. John Redfield, interview II, 24–25.
334. Ibid., 14.
335. Swann, interview, 12.
336. Louise Levy, interview II, 5–8.
337. Louise Levy, interview I, 3–4.
338. Swann, interview, 8.
339. Neandross, interview, 9–10.

340. Louise Levy, interview I, 17.
341. John Redfield, interview II, 20.
342. John Redfield's Baby Book, Baby's First Journey.
343. *The Tenakin 1926*, 29–30.
344. Ibid., 16, 99.
345. Ibid., 7
346. *The Tenakin 1927*, 24.
347. John Redfield's Baby Book, A Record of Birthdays page
348. Louise Levy, interview II, 23.
349. *The Tenakin 1927*, 15.
350. Louise Redfield's Baby Book, First Lesson.
351. Ibid., Mother's Notes.
352. Ibid., First Lesson.
353. Louise Levy, interview I, 15.
354. Louise Redfield's Baby Book, Important Events.
355. Ibid., First Lesson.
356. Swann, interview, 8.
357. Louise Levy, interview I, 24.
358. Ibid., 15.
359. Louise Levy, interview II, 2.
360. Louise Levy, interview I, 25.
361. John Redfield, interview I, 21.
362. Neandross, interview, 6.
363. Ibid., 5.
364. Louise Levy, interview I, 24.
365. Louise Levy, interview II, 16.
366. Dumont Clarke III, interview, 14.

18. Floating University

367. Grace, "History of Shipboard Education."
368. Caption on Floating University press photo from original voyage, June 14, 1927, author's collection.
369. *Floating University Bulletin* 2, no. 3 (January 1929): 2,
370. Floating University pamphlet, *Itinerary and Academic Calendar*, n.d.
371. Lucy Bancroft, letter to her mother, November ??, 1928.
372. John Redfield, interview I, 19.
373. Lucy Bancroft, letter to her family, December 25, 1928.
374. Lucy Bancroft, letter to her mother, March 7, 1929.
375. Lucy Bancroft, letter to her family, February 4, 1929.

376. Lucy Bancroft, letter to her mother, February 14, 1929.
377. Ibid.
378. Ibid., February 18, 1929.
379. Ibid.
380. Ibid., February 29, 1929.
381. Lucy Bancroft, letter to her family, March 6, 1929.
382. Lucy Bancroft, letter to her mother, March 7, 1929.
383. Ibid., March 20, 1929.
384. Ibid., March 25, 1929.
385. Ibid., March 31, 1929.
386. Ibid., April 18, 1929.
387. Ibid., April 24, 1929.
388. Ibid., May 8, 1929.
389. Lucy Bancroft, letter to her father, May 7, 1929.
390. Lucy Bancroft, letter to her mother, May 8, 1929.
391. Ibid., May 16, 1929.
392. Ibid., May 17, 1929,
393. *San Francisco Examiner* clipping, n.d., of an article with a dateline of Paris, May 21, 1929, reprinted from the *Chicago Tribune*.
394. Lucy Bancroft, letter to her mother, May 29, 1929.
395. Ibid., June 8, 1929.
396. Floating University newsletter, "A Message from President Greenbie," n.d., early 1929.
397. Unidentified publication, advertisement for the Fifth Floating University, November 15, 1930.

19. Changing Times, Changing Lives

398. Swann, interview, 22.
399. Neandross, interview, 12.
400. Louise Levy, interview I, 4.
401. Swann, interview, 22–23.
402. Raymond, interview, 16.
403. MacKay, letter to Alice Redfield, July 10, 1931.
404. Dennis, letter to Alice Redfield, January 14, 1933.
405. Neandross, interview, 12.
406. John Redfield, interview II, 21.
407. John Redfield, interview I, 16.
408. Swann, interview, 11.
409. John Redfield, interview III, 5.

410. John Redfield, interview I, 5.
411. *Tenafly Suburbanite*, obituary, Lucy Redfield, June 16, 1971.
412. John Redfield, interview III, 8.
413. *The Tenakin 1933*, 28.
414. Louise Levy, interview II, 19.
415. John Redfield, interview III, 9.
416. John Redfield, interview I, 17.
417. *The Tenakin 1935*, 30.
418. Louise Levy, interview I, 22–23.
419. Laurence Levy, interview, 10.
420. Henry Redfield, carbon copy of a note to Julia Russell, June 15, 1930.
421. John Redfield, interview II, 17.
422. Louise Levy, interview I, 18.
423. John Redfield, interview II, 16–17.
424. Louise Levy, interview II, 4.
425. Ibid., 3.
426. Fisher, *Story of the Mary Fisher Home*.
427. Rigney and Stefanowicz, *Tenafly*, 74.
428. Louise Levy, interview I, 25.
429. Louise Levy, interview II, 4–5.
430. Ibid., 1.
431. Ager, *We Plow God's Fields*, 350.
432. Dumont Clarke III, interview, 3.
433. Louise Levy, interview II, 19.
434. Raymond, interview, 17.

20. Weddings West and East

435. Louise Levy, interview II, 8.
436. Lucy Bancroft, letter to John Redfield, May 5, 1935.
437. Louise Levy, interview I, 5–6.
438. John Redfield, interview I, 5.
439. *Berkley California Gazette*, Redfield-Bancroft Wedding, August 22, 1935.
440. *San Francisco News*, "Miss Lucy Bancroft, Bride of John A. Redfield," August 21, 1935.
441. Louise Levy, interview II, 25.
442. Ibid.
443. Neandross, interview, 13.
444. Dorothy Redfield, interview, 4.
445. Louise Levy, interview I, 11.

446. *The Tenakin 1934*, 26.
447. Laurence Levy, 4.
448. Louise Levy, interview II, 9.

21. Settling Down

449. Louise Levy, interview II, 3–4.
450. Louise Levy, interview I, 17.
451. Louise Levy, interview II, 1.
452. Ibid., 3.
453. Phillip Bancroft Sr., letter to Lucy Bancroft Redfield, June 21, 1937.
454. Unidentified newspaper, handwriting analysis, A.R.C., Tenafly, June 1937.
455. Lucy Bancroft, letter to John Redfield, August 6, 1935.
456. Laurence Levy, interview, 7.
457. Dorothy Redfield, interview, 2.
458. John Redfield, genealogical notes.
459. Dorothy Redfield, interview, 2.
460. Louise Levy, interview I, 9.
461. Ibid., 23.
462. Ibid., 6.
463. Ibid., 10.
464. Ibid., 6–7.
465. John Redfield, genealogical notes.

22. Reaching the End

466. John Redfield, genealogical notes
467. Louise Levy, interview II, 10.
468. Ibid., 11.
469. Ibid., 12.
470. Ibid., 12–13.
471. Ibid., 12.
472. *Northern Valley Tribune*, "Tenafly Pays Tribute to Mrs. Henry W. Redfield, Prominent Civic Leader," May 14, 1943.

23. Afterward

473. Louise Levy, interview II, 13.
474. John Redfield, genealogical notes.

475. Laurence Levy, interview, 12.
476. Dumont Clarke III, interview, 13.

24. Why Was Alice Short?

477. Genetics Home Reference, "Isolated Growth Hormone Deficiency," 1.
478. Ibid., 2–3.
479. Sullivan, *Tom Thumb*, 168.
480. *New York Times*, "Death of Minnie Warren," July 24, 1878.
481. Grzeskowiak-Krwawicz, *Gulliver in the Land of Giants*, 7.
482. Ibid., 29.

BIBLIOGRAPHY

Articles

Cragin, Edwin B. "Cesarean Section." *Obstetrical and Gynecological Reports Volume 1*, Ward, Wilbur, MD., Editor. Sloan Hospital for Women New York City (1913): 13–19.

———. "The Sloan Hospital for Women." *Obstetrical and Gynecological Reports Volume 1*, Ward, Wilbur, MD. Editor. Sloan Hospital for Women New York City (1913): 5–12.

———. "Treatment of Ectopic Gestation." O*bstetrical and Gynecological Reports Volume 1*, edited by Ward, Wilbur, MD. Editor. Sloan Hospital for Women New York City (1913): 66–77.

Grace, Michael L. "A History of Shipboard Education—MV Explorer—1910–2010." Cruising the Past. February 25, 2010. cruiselinehistory.com.

The Historian. "The Story of the U.S.A. Base Hospital at Camp Merritt, N.J." Pts. 1 and 2. *The Mess Kit* 1, no. 1 (March 1919); 1, no. 2 (April 1919).

Redfield, Alice. Baby book entries for her son Clarke, handwritten, titled and untitled pages, various dates (partial copy, Xeroxed).

Redfield, Alice: Baby Book entries for her son John, handwritten, titled and untitled pages, various dates.

Redfield, Alice: Baby Book entries for her daughter Louise, handwritten, titled and untitled pages, various dates (partial copy, Xeroxed).

Wikipedia. "Dwight-Englewood School." Last modified January 20, 2020. https://en.wikipedia.org/wiki/Dwight-Englewood_School.

———. "Heidelberg Tun." Last modified November 6, 2019. https://en.wikipedia.org/wiki/Heidelberg_Tun.

———. "Lakewood Township." Last modified December 17, 2019. https://en.wikipedia.org/wiki/Lakewood_Township%2C_New_Jersey.

———. "Plymouth Brethren." Last modified October 1, 2019. https://en.wikipedia.org/wiki/Plymouth_Brethren.

———. "United States in World War I." Last modified January 22, 2020. https://en.wikipedia.org/wiki/United_States_in_World_War_I.

Booklets and Pamphlets

Camp Merritt. 1924.

Camp Merrit the Camp Beautiful. N.p., n.d.

Merritt Hall, The Soldier's Club. Camp Merritt, NJ, 1919.

Books

Ager, John Curtis. *We Plow God's Fields.* Boone, NC: Appalachian Consortium Press, Boone, 1991.

Altschuler, H. Jean. *Dumont Heritage.* Old Schraalenburgh, NJ: Borough of Dumont, 1969.

Andrews, F. Emerson. *The Tenafly Public Library, A History: 1891–1970.* Tenafly, NJ: Free Public Library of the Borough of Tenafly, 1970.

Bartholf, Howard E. *Camp Merritt.* Charleston, SC: Arcadia Publishing, 2017.

Baum, Willa K. *Oral History for the Local Historical Society*, 2nd rev. ed. Nashville, TN: American Association for State and Local History, 1971.

Clarke, Alice Coe. Diary, 1900.

———. Diary, 1902.

———. European Trip Diary, 1903.

Clarke, E. Stanley. Diary. *My Long Sail on the Big Blue Sea, November 15, 1894–March 13, 1896, on the* S.P. Hitchcock.

Fisher, Mary A. *The Story of the Mary Fisher Home.* N.p.: F.B. & C. Ltd., 2015.

Grzeskowiak-Krwawicz, Anna. *Gulliver in the Land of Giants: A Critical Biography and the Memoirs of the Celebrated Dwarf Joseph Boruwlaski.* Translated by Daniel Sax. Burlington, VT: Ashgate Publishing, 2012.

Magri, Countess M. Lavinia, formerly Mrs. General Tom Thumb, with the assistance of Sylvester Bleeker. *The Autobiography of Mrs. Tom Thumb (Some of My Life Experiences).* Edited and introduced by A.H. Saxon. Hamden, CT: Archon Books, Hamden, 1979.

Morrison, George Austin, Jr. *The Clarke Families of Rhode Island.* New York: Press of the Evening Post Job Printing House, 1902. Reprinted by Higginson Book Company, Salem, Massachusetts.

Page, Nick. *Lord Minimus, The Extraordinary Life of Britain's Smallest Man.* New York: St. Martins Press, 2001.

Redfield, John Howard. *Genealogical History of the Redfield Family in the United States.* Allyn, WA: Barbara Ann Redfield, 1988. First published 1860 by Munsell & Rowland, Albany, C.B. Richardson (New York).

Rigney, Alice Renner. *Tenafly's Unidentified Photographer.* Limited edition private publication, 2010.

Rigney, Alice Renner, and Paul J. Stefanowicz. *Tenafly.* Charleston, SC: Arcadia Publishing, 2009.

Speert, Harold, MD. *The Sloan Hospital Chronicle.* Philadelphia: F.A. Davis Company, 1963.

Sullivan, George. *Tom Thumb, The Remarkable True Story of a Man in Miniature.* Boston: Clarion Books, 2011.

The Tenakin 1926. Tenafly, NJ: Tenafly High School, 1926.

The Tenakin 1927. Tenafly, NJ: Tenafly High School, 1927.

The Tenakin 1933. Tenafly, NJ: Tenafly High School, 1933.

The Tenakin 1934. Tenafly, NJ: Tenafly High School, 1934.

The Tenakin 1935. Tenafly, NJ: Tenafly High School, 1935.

Thoms, Herbert, MD. *Our Obstetric Heritage, The Story of Safe Childbirth.* Hamden, CT: Shoestring Press, 1960.

Trowbridge, Carolyn. *Andrew Taylor Still, 1828–1917.* Kirksville, MO: Truman State University Press, 1991.

Interviews

Clarke, Dumont III. Interview, February 29, 1980.

Levy, Laurence. Interview, February 27, 1980.

Levy, Louise Redfield. Interview I, February 21, 1980.

———. Interview II, March 1, 1980.

Neandross, Katherine Stillman. Interview, February 29, 1980.

Raymond, Frances. Interview, February 27, 1980.

Redfield, Dorothy Z. Interview February 29, 1980.

Redfield, John A. Interview I, February 26, 1980.

———. Interview II, March 2, 1980.

———. Interview III, December 26, 1981.

Swann, Katherine Wadham. Interview, February 27, 1980.

Letters

Bancroft, Lucy. Series of letters to her family describing the third voyage of the Floating University, 1928–29.

———. Letter to John Redfield, May 5, 1935.

———. Letter to John Redfield, August 6, 1935.

Bancroft, Phillip Sr. Letter to Lucy Bancroft Redfield, June 21, 1937.

Cabois, H. Letter to Alice Clarke, September 17, 1903.

Case, George. Letter to Alice Clarke, October 28, 1897.

———. Letter to Alice Clarke, November 4, 1897.

Clarke, Alice, and Fanny Clarke. Letter to Cornelia Clarke, August 14, 1886.

Clarke, Corinne. Letter to Alice and Henry Redfield, January 21, 1904.

Clarke, Cornelia. Letter to Alice Clarke, March 3, 1893.

———. Letter to Alice Clarke, May 16, 1893.

———. Letter to Alice Redfield, January 24, 1904.

———. Letter to Alice Redfield, July 22, 1906.

Clarke, Dumont Jr. Letter to Alice Redfield, August 3, 1906.

———. Letter from India, "The Work of the YMCA," 1907.

———. Letter from India, December 24, 1907.

———. Letter, "Diseases of Southern India," March 12, 1908.

———. Letter to Alice Redfield, March 14, 1910.

Clarke, Dumont Sr. Letter to Alice Redfield, September 20, 1909.

———. Letter to Alice Redfield, October 25, 1909.

Clarke, Ernest. Letter to Alice Clarke from Bielefeld, Germany, October 5, 1896.

———. Letter to Alice Clarke from Bielefeld, Germany, November 2, 1896.

Clarke, Stanley. Letter to Alice Clarke, February 16, 1890.

Dennis, N.M.F., Clerk, Tenafly Board of Education. Letter to Alice Redfield, January 14, 1933.

Ellery, Elizabeth Martin. Letter, December 30, 1886.

Mackay, Malcolm S. Letter to Alice Redfield, July 10, 1931.

Raymond, Jessie Clarke. Letter to Alice, July 20, 1901.

Redfield, Henry W. Jr. Letter to Alice Clarke, September 19, 1902.

———. Letter to Alice Clarke, September 23, 1902.

———. Letter to Alice Clarke, January 19, 1904.

———. Letter to Julia Russell, June 15, 1930.

Redfield, Henry W. Sr., Letter to his daughter Louise Redfield, September 29, 1880.

Redfield, John A. Note, n.d.

Redfield, Lavinia. Letter to Henry Redfield Jr., January 24, 1904.

Redfield, Louise. Letter to Alice Redfield, May 5, 1915.

Redfield, Richard W. Letter to Susan Jane Lowerre, August 31, 1843.

Woodward, Eugene. Letters to Alice, December 1, 1895, and December 15, 1895.

Newspaper Clippings

Bergen County Record. "Tenafly Council Meeting." January 5, 1918.

Berkley California Gazette. "Redfield-Bancroft Wedding." August 22, 1935.

New York Commercial. "A Type of Successful New Yorker—Dumont Clarke." April 4, 1902.

New York Herald. "Lakewood's Tiniest Bride." January 23, 1904.

New York Times. "Case—Clarke." March 3, 1898.

———. "Death of George S. Coe." May 4, 1896.

———. "Death of Minnie Warren." July 24, 1878.

———. "Dumont Clarke Buys Yacht *Kalolah*." May 13, 1903.

———. "Dumont Clarke Dies at 69, of Pneumonia." December 27, 1909.

———. "Dumont Clarke a Pastor." January 1, 1911.

———. "Dumont Clarke Sells the *Tranquilo*." May 9, 1903.

———. "Ex-Mayor Low's Yacht Sold." April 2, 1904.

———. "Many Changes at National Banks." January 10, 1894.

———. "Mrs. Dumont Clarke Dead." March 16, 1908.

———. Obituary, Dumont Clarke. December 27, 1909.

Northern Valley Tribune. "Tenafly Pays Tribute to Mrs. Henry W. Redfield, Prominent Civic Leader." May 14, 1943.

San Francisco News. "Miss Lucy Bancroft, Bride of John A. Redfield." August 21, 1935.

Tenafly Record. "Alice Redfield Returns Home." March 30, 1907.

———. "Redfield—Clarke." January 23, 1904.

Tenafly Suburbanite. Obituary for Lucy Bancroft Redfield. June 16, 1971.

Unidentified. A.R.C.—Tenafly, handwriting analysis. June 1937 .

———. "Human Caravan, Gold Laden, Halts Traffic in Broadway Near Cedar Street Twice Daily." 1899.

———. "Lewis L. Clarke Takes Father's Post in Bank." January 12, 1910.

———. "Wedding Bells Redfield-Dakin." October 20, 1897.

Other Materials

Bordentown Female College. blank receipt; postcard, undated; tuition bill 1864.

Clarke, Dumont Sr. Last Will and Testament, May 9, 1902; First Codicil, September 15, 1903; Second Codicil, January 29, 1909.

Floating University Bulletin 2, no. 3 (January 1929).

Genetics Home Reference, National Institutes of Health. "Isolated Growth Hormone Deficiency." Published January 21, 2020. http://ghr.nlm.nih.gov/condition/isolated-growth-hormone-deficiency.

Redfield, Clarke. Baptismal Certificate, July 23, 1907.

Redfield, John. Notes on Family Genealogy. n.d.

Redfield, Louise. "Behind the Headlines." Term paper, Goucher College, Towson, MD, November 24, 1936.

Sloan Hospital for Women. Infant Patient Record for Louise Redfield, May 1, 1815.

———. "Recommended Infant Feeding List." 1907.

State of New Jersey. Marriage Certificate, Henry Wells Redfield Jr., Alice Coe Clarke, January 20, 1904.

ABOUT THE AUTHOR

Judy Redfield earned a master's degree in physical anthropology from Harvard, completed everything but the thesis for her doctorate and decided she would rather raise a family than be an academic. For entertainment on weekends, she started attending country auctions and found so many interesting bargains she decided to open an antique shop.

She operated that business on the side for the next thirty years. Along the way she became fascinated with American Victorian Silverplate and, with Dorothy Rainwater, coauthored the fourth edition of the latter's *Encyclopedia of American Silver Manufacturers*. When forced by circumstances to take over the family financial management business, the antiques business was phased out.

Judy first learned about Alice Redfield when she married in 1966. She made periodic inquiries of family members about Alice over the next few years. When she learned of the work of Willa Baum, a pioneer in the oral history field who had interviewed another relative, she decided to try the same approach herself. Alice's daughter, Louise Redfield Levy, and her brother, John Alden Redfield, got together and organized a series of interviews for her with relatives and a family friend in early 1980. Louise loaned her numerous items to copy as well. Judy's husband's serious illness in early 1981 put the project on hold, and she was unable to get back to it until recently.

Visit us at
www.historypress.com